Sermon Treks

Sermon Treks

Trailways to Creative Preaching

Ronald J. Allen

Abingdon Press
Nashville

Library of Congress Cataloging-in-Publication Data

Allen, Ronald J. (Ronald James), 1949-
    Sermon treks : trailways to creative preaching / Ronald J. Allen.
    pages cm.
    ISBN 978-1-4267-6386-1 (alk. paper)
1. Preaching.   I. Title.
    BV4211.3.A453 2013
    251—dc23
                                                            2013030847

13 14 15 16 17 18 19 20 21 22—10 9 8 7 6 5 4 3 2 1
MANUFACTURED IN THE UNITED STATES OF AMERICA

To

Emily SerVaas Allen

and

Elisha Montgomery Robb

Creative Additions to our Family Trek

CONTENTS

INTRODUCTION

Every preacher picking up this book has likely heard (or made) comments similar to the following.

- "I can't believe how texts in the lectionary match up so well with the situation in our congregation right now." (From a lectionary preacher)

- "I have sat in front of this blank screen for hours, but nothing is coming. The lectionary readings just don't connect." (From a lectionary preacher)

- "The lectionary is the only way I can imagine preaching." (From a lectionary preacher)

- "I wanted to address a particular issue in our congregation, so I put together a sermon series and attendance increased every week." (From a non-lectionary preacher)

- "I love the freedom to choose a biblical passage every week from which to preach. But the other day, someone asked, 'Why do you preach so much from the book of Acts? The Bible is much bigger.'" (From a non-lectionary preacher)

- "I can't imagine why any preacher would become prisoner of the lectionary." (From a non-lectionary preacher)

These comments point to the strange situation of many preachers. On the one hand, I know preachers who are drawn to the Christian year and the *Revised Common Lectionary* as starting points for preaching, and for whom the Christian year and the lectionary often generate homiletical heat that bursts into flame in the sermon.[1] Still, some weeks the Christian year and the RCL leave these preachers in the cold without shoes or a sweater. On the other hand, I know preachers who, from Sunday to Sunday, prefer to choose their own texts and set up their own sermon series, but whose homiletical well becomes shallow and runs dry. They often wonder, "Where do I turn this week?"

This book seeks to provide practical help in these matters by mapping a wide range of trailways to the sermon and by helping the preacher identify the strengths and cautions of each. These evaluative remarks function like trail markers that help the hiker anticipate what kind of terrain is ahead and what kind of equipment is needed to navigate it.

Rather than try to persuade the reader that one pathway to the sermon fits all congregations and contexts, the book encourages the preacher to become familiar with a range of starting points for sermon preparation and to think critically about which pathways have good chances of helping the congregation come to life-shaping interpretations of God and God's purposes at particular moments in the congregation's life.

A Shift to the Christian Year and the Revised Common Lectionary

During the first seventy-five years of the twentieth century, many preachers in historic Protestant denominations begin their sermon preparation by freely selecting individual biblical texts, preaching continuously through books of the Bible, preaching topical sermons, and turning to sermon series. Such churches observed Christmas and Easter while also frequently lifting up Mother's Day, Memorial Day, Fourth of July, Labor Day, Thanksgiving, and other days in the civic calendar. A part of the church's calendar was thus determined by civic life. Indeed, this was the kind of preaching on which I grew up and which was commonplace in many congregations when I was ordained in 1974.

Through much of the twentieth century, the Roman Catholic Church observed the Christian year and read from a lectionary, but Roman Catholic preaching was often centered more in church teaching than in the Bible. Among long-established Protestant churches, the Christian year and lectionaries were largely the province of Episcopal and Lutheran bodies, with some Reformed churches taking a similar path.

The Second Vatican Council (1962–1965) in the Roman Catholic Church set in motion a pattern of liturgical reform that was soon taken up by many ministers and congregations in historic Protestant churches. This pattern, called the *ecumenical consensus in worship,* orders the worship life

2

of a congregation around the seasons of the Christian year (Advent, Christmas, Epiphany Day, Lent, Easter, Pentecost Day, and Ordinary Time). Individual services follow a historic form of worship that begins with the community *gathering, confessing sin,* then *reading the Bible and hearing the sermon.* The congregation *responds,* often with an affirmation of faith, a time of prayer, or both. The community makes an *offering,* particularly of bread and cup, and the service reaches its climax in the *Sacred Meal,* after which the community *goes forth* to extend the service of word and table into service in the everyday world.[2]

Two developments are key for preaching. First, many Roman Catholic and Protestant leaders in preaching concluded that the sermon should begin with the interpretation of a biblical text.[3] In the Roman Catholic Church, this turn meant that the sermon should no longer focus so much on church teaching but should originate in the exposition of the Bible. On the Protestant side, the biblical emphasis meant that topical sermons fell into disfavor. Moreover the preacher was expected to deal with the text exegetically and theologically and not simply to use the text as a springboard into what the preacher wanted to say.

Second, in 1969 the Roman Catholic Church published a table of Bible readings (a lectionary) coordinated with the major themes of the Christian year as the starting point for sermon preparation. Several Protestant churches took up this initiative. By 1978, the Consultation on Common Texts was under way, with both Catholics and Protestants involved, to establish a shared (common) body of readings. In 1983, this group published the *Common Lectionary.*[4] In response to critical reflection on almost a decade of use, the Consultation published a follow-up version in 1993, the *Revised Common Lectionary* (RCL).[5] Ever since, significant numbers of ministers, priests, and congregations in the historic churches (and some beyond) have used the RCL in the context of the Christian year.

Cheers for the Lectionary: Three, Two, One, None, and Boo

The venerable David Buttrick of Vanderbilt Divinity School says, "Two Cheers and Some Questions" for the RCL.[6] In my view a preacher could sometimes give three cheers, sometimes two, sometimes one, and sometimes none. Indeed, occasionally a preacher should boo the lectionary.

On the one hand, as noted previously, I welcome aspects of the shift to lectionary preaching for many of the reasons given in chapter 2. Indeed, the RCL offers so much that I have coauthored a three-volume commentary on the lectionary, calling attention to the Jewishness of lectionary passages while imploring preachers to avoid anti-Judaism when dealing with negative pictures of Jewish people and institutions.[7] I have recently joined two colleagues in editing a three-volume commentary on the RCL from the perspective of social justice.[8] I was part of a team that urged congregations in our movement—the Christian Church (Disciples of Christ)—toward the Christian year and the *Revised Common Lectionary*.[9] For almost forty years I have written page after page of commentary on lectionary readings for various periodicals focused on lectionary preaching. My homiletical GPS has been set so that I follow the Christian year and the RCL.

Conversation with the theological themes of the Christian year and the biblical texts of the RCL is, indeed, sometimes a rich and deep path for helping a congregation come to a believable interpretation of the presence and mission of God in a particular context. In thinking critically about the Christian year and the *Revised Common Lectionary,* I do not take cheap shots from afar.

On the other hand, the Christian year and the RCL have never quite become a part of my ecclesial soul. The same is true for some other preachers and congregations familiar to me, including some who have followed this path for many years. I have tried and tried to socialize myself into the Christian year and the RCL. At certain moments and seasons, these approaches to preaching do feel like home. But at other times the Christian year and the RCL seem distant, disconnected, and even alienated from my world. Sometimes they get in the way of coming to a vital interpretation of God's aims. Indeed, aspects of the Christian year and the *Revised Common Lectionary* run against the grain of some of my deepest theological convictions. When I have voiced such ambiguities with other preachers, I have been surprised at how many share similar sentiments.

Other ways of launching sermon preparation sometimes seem more timely and potent in their promise to help the congregation toward lifegiving interpretations of the presence and purposes of the living God. I think, for example, of preaching through books of the Bible, preaching from biblical themes, developing sermon series, freely selecting texts, and yes, preaching topical sermons. Preaching that begins from such places can help congregations interpret the presence and purposes of God in particular contexts. Of course, since human finitude is pervasive, preachers and congregations can lose their way while following these approaches.

Since I am a member of one of the long-established (but now declining) denominations, I am particularly concerned with the renewal of preaching in such congregations. However, I believe this book will be of interest to preachers in churches across the historical and theological spectra.

Different Equipment for Different Treks

I grew up on the edge of the Ozark Mountains, where a trek usually meant hiking, canoeing, or biking. I have since trekked in the Blue Ridge Mountains in Georgia, in the Rocky Mountains in New Mexico and Colorado, on Mount Hood in Oregon, in the rain forests of Jamaica and Belize, across part of the desert in Israel, and along the Zambezi River in Zambia. The treks are similar in that they all involve journeying toward significant destinations. Yet each trek is different. Some involve straining every muscle climbing steep inclines, and others lead to sweating like a water faucet opened wide while plodding through steamy fields. Others include shooting down rapids in a canoe at risk of careening out of control, and still others entail baking under the naked sun. Trekkers need different maps, clothing, equipment, and supplies for different treks. With the best gear chosen for each journey ahead, trekkers hope every adventure adds to their lives and brings them to a point where something good happens.

The trek life is a good way of speaking about preaching. Going from the starting point of sermon preparation to the sermon and its afterglow is a kind of theological and pastoral trek. Congregations are in places as different as the Ozarks, the Rockies, the rain forests, the desert, and the Zambezi. Indeed, the spiritual ecology of one congregation can be as different over time as those different kinds of geographies and treks. This means that preachers need different kinds of homiletical maps, theological equipment, and hermeneutical supplies. They pack what they need for the terrain. The canoe that was just right for the rapids on the Current River in the Ozarks would not have been so helpful trekking across the Sinai.

To use more traditional theological language, postmodern emphases on diversity, particularity, and otherness come into play. As noted earlier, a fundamental purpose of preaching is to help the congregation interpret and respond to the presence and purposes of the living God. A preacher needs to approach the sermon from a starting point that gives the preacher a good chance of generating a conversation with the congregation that will help the community move toward a theologically adequate interpretation of the situation in which the sermon comes to life. This is the heart of the distinctive and irreplaceable work of preachers who have critical pastoral insight into their congregations and contexts. Scholars in disparate places like Boston, New Haven, New York, Princeton, Durham, Chicago, Decatur, Dallas, Claremont, and Berkeley cannot make such decisions for the preacher in the congregation on Main Street.

While the preacher needs to select promising starting points from

5

individual sermon to individual sermon, O. Wesley Allen Jr., a leading scholar of preaching, stresses that preaching can have optimum cumulative effects when the themes of sermons work together over a long arc of time.[10] Not only from week to week but from season to season and from year to year, the preacher needs to select starting points that help nourish the congregation's theological perception and response.

The Social and Theological Location of the Writer

Contemporary theologians stress that the social location of preacher and congregation often contributes to what preacher and people see and seek in the Bible, in theology, in ecclesial life, and in ethical behavior.[11] Social location is the thick interweaving of the factors that make up a life: gender, sex, race, ethnicity, social experience, class, education, political commitments, geographical location, community setting, and philosophical and religious viewpoints. Individuals and groups often seek to interpret Christian tradition in ways that benefit their social locations. Preachers need to reflect critically on how our social locations affect what we would like to find in the Bible and Christian theology, in the life and witness of the church, in what we think the sermon should be, and in interpreting God's purposes for the larger world.

In keeping with this emphasis, it is only fair that the reader of this book have access to the author's social location. Raised in a small town on the edge of the Ozark Mountains in southern Missouri, I grew up in a large and vibrant congregation of the Christian Church (Disciples of Christ). Our church was marked by the doctrine of justification by grace, seeking unity among Christians, impatience with creeds, rational preaching, baptism of believers by immersion, weekly gathering for the Sacred Meal, and freedom of theological interpretation. One of our slogans was, "In essentials unity, in nonessentials liberty, and in all things charity [love]." These elements continue to loom large in my consciousness. I try not to let them predetermine where my preaching and scholarship go, but the reader will see them in this book in both surface and hidden ways.

Beyond that, I am a middle-class, heterosexual male of Eurocentric origin, married for more than thirty-eight years to a clergywoman with whom I raised five children. My spouse serves as minister of the West Street Christian Church (Disciples of Christ) in Tipton, Indiana, where I am active. I have taught preaching and Gospels and Letters at Christian Theological Seminary for more than thirty years, and I can hardly believe the seminary pays me to do what I would want to do anyway.

By way of theological orientation, I subscribe to process (relational) theology. I believe in a God of unconditional love, who seeks for all people to live together in love. While God has more power than any other entity, God does not have the unilateral power to interrupt and reshape situations. I believe divine power is exercised through lure. Many people find these views unsatisfactory, but they help me make sense of God, the world, and real-life experience.

I like to find things in the Bible and Christian tradition and theology that support my place in the world and my theological, social, and political views. I need to listen critically to others—to people and viewpoints that call into question my social location and theological perspectives.

I regard preaching as a conversation in which the preacher helps the congregation listen to how others interpret the presence and purposes of God while encouraging the congregation toward its own adequate understanding of these things.[12] The others to whom the preacher turns include the Bible, the history of the church, Christian theology, the congregation, individuals and communities outside the Christian house, the multiple forms of knowledge available in our time, and others in the purview of the sermon. While most preachers *assume* the authority of the Bible and Christian tradition, I am persuaded that other voices, and even those from outside the Bible and Christian community, can sometimes challenge not only particular interpretations of the Bible and Christian theology but aspects of the Bible and doctrine themselves.

New Names for the Old Book: Torah, Prophets, Writings, Gospels, Letters

I have long been on a journey with others seeking more satisfactory terms for the parts of the Bible than Old Testament and New Testament. While the notion of *old* in antiquity often invoked respect for things of the past, the word *old* today frequently bespeaks things that are worn out. Contemporary North American culture is addicted to the new, often in replacement of the old. Whether intended or not, this language contributes to Christians sometimes diminishing the Old Testament, regarding it as second class, worn out, or even in need of replacement. The New Testament, by contrast, is perceived to be the new and improved part of the Bible.

Having considered other terms, such as Hebrew Bible, Greek Scriptures, Christian Scriptures, and First and Second Testaments, I am now exploring Torah, Prophets, Writings, Gospels, and Letters as names for parts of the Bible.[13] This nomenclature builds on a Jewish pattern suggested in the acronym Tanakh, a name the Jewish community sometimes uses for their Bible: Torah

(Torah), Nevi'im (prophets), and Ketuvim (writings). The Gospels and Letters continue the story that began in the Torah, Prophets, and Writings.

Chapters Highlight Different Treks for Preaching

This book begins with a survey of the Christian year as a context for preaching (chapter 1). The next chapters describe the Revised Common Lectionary and identify strengths and cautions of following that trailway to sermon (chapters 2 and 3). Chapter 4 deals with preaching through a book of the Bible. Chapter 5 lifts up the African American Lectionary and other cultural and civic lectionary impulses. Chapter 6 turns to the chronology of major biblical events as well as schools of thought within the Bible as trailheads for preaching. Chapter 7 looks at sermon series that start with biblical texts or themes. Chapter 8 adds preaching from doctrines, practices, and personal and social issues to the preacher's homiletical backpack. Chapter 9 ends the book by considering sermons that come from the free selection of biblical texts from week to week.

I intend to show respect and fairness for all viewpoints discussed in this book. As long as we are this side of the full and final manifestation of the realm of God, we are finite and our perception is relative. In such a state, we can at least be civil and fair.

Sermon Treks Lead to Life-Giving Vistas

A recent trek comes to mind as an analogy of what can happen on the trailway to the pulpit. Our family—two sixty-something parents, five young adult children, and two young adult spouses—camped in an eco-setting in the Caribbean. One morning, to see the sunrise over the sea, we got up at 4:00 a.m. and hiked through the rain forest up a mountain, negotiating bushes, boulders, ravines, briars, logs, and ruins, not to mention the dark. For this trek we needed thick hats, strong lights, steel-toed shoes, a compass, and a son-in-law with an unerring sense of direction.

When we reached the top, the surrounding ocean and forest were wrapped in fog. But as the sun rose, the fog rolled up like a scroll, and we were bathed in as pure a moment as I can remember. We saw each other and the world in new ways.

Every sermon will not reach such a height. But if the preacher has negotiated the trek in a way that is appropriate to God, time, and place, the preacher and the congregation alike will see more clearly through the fog of life.

CHAPTER 1

Preaching from the Christian Year

The names of the seasons of the Christian year sometimes captivate early twenty-first-century people: Advent, Christmas, Epiphany Day, Ordinary Time, Lent, Easter, Pentecost Day, and Ordinary Time. These names imply connections with the past while prompting the mind to imagine what they might mean for the present. The colors of the Christian year enliven the worship space even as they symbolize themes: purple or light blue (Advent), white (Christmas and Epiphany Day), green (Ordinary Time), purple (Lent), white (Easter), and red (Pentecost Day). At the same time, these names can seem out of place. "How do you pronounce that word—*Epiphany*? And what does it mean?" Congregations are sometimes conflicted about the Christian year. I would like to have a dollar for every time I have heard about a congregational disagreement over whether to sing Christmas carols during Advent.

This chapter first briefly sketches the origin and development of the Christian year. I describe theology and functions of the Christian year with attention to how the major seasons and days affect preaching. The chapter concludes with strengths and weaknesses of the Christian year as a starting point for preaching.

While the Christian year and the *Revised Common Lectionary* are usually interwoven in today's church, the Christian year does not require the lectionary. A preacher can follow the main themes of the Christian year without following the RCL.

A Brief History of the Christian Year

We turn to history because history helps us understand the originating purposes and evolution of events, ideas, and practices.[1] We can then think critically about the degree to which those purposes are appropriate for today.

Many liturgical scholars think that in early human history, human beings began to worship in response to events that suggested the presence of a transcendent power, such as a dramatic occurrence in nature that aroused awe. People worshiped spontaneously when such events occurred to acknowledge the presence of the transcendent power.

After the event passed, communities developed acts of worship to rekindle the feelings of awe and to live in harmony with that power. Liturgy helped ancient communities answer fundamental questions of life. Who are we in relationship to the transcendent power? How are we to live? Regular worship helped recall the presence of the transcendent and appropriate response.

The Roots of the Christian Year in Judaism

Such themes were in the background of the worship of the Jewish community. While liturgical scholars debate how worship emerged among the Hebrews, it seems likely that before the exodus from Egypt, the Hebrew people observed agricultural festivals to maintain relationship with the God of Sarah and Abraham as the guarantor of their life. After the exodus, many communities added the deliverance from Egypt to the people's essential memory.

By the exile (597 to 538 BCE), many Jewish people regarded the Sabbath as a centerpiece of Jewish life. We find differences of emphasis here. The priestly theologians emphasize that God rested on the Sabbath and gave the human family the Sabbath as a day of rest (Gen. 2:1-4; Exod. 20:8-11). The life of Israel—and the life of the world—are to reflect the way God lives. The Deuteronomistic theologians emphasize Sabbath as both a day of rest and a day to remember the deliverance from Egypt (Deut. 5:12-15).[2] The Passover and the Feast of Unleavened Bread (Exod. 12:1–13:10, esp. 13:5-10; 23:14-17; Lev. 23:6-8; Num. 28:17-25) became important for many communities, as did other major festivals, such as the Waving of the Sheaf (Lev. 23:9-14), Weeks (Lev. 23:15-21; Num. 28:26-31), and Booths (Lev. 23:33-36; Num. 29:12-38). By the Hellenistic period (300 BCE to 200 CE), some communities added Purim and Hanukkah to the liturgical calendar (Esth. 3:7; 9:14; 1 Macc. 4:59; 2 Macc. 10:6-8). As the Jewish community evolved, so did its worship.

Both the priestly and Deuteronomistic theological families wrote around the time of the exile, when Jewish life and identity were threatened. The Hellenistic Jewish theologians wrote when the community lived in a vise with one prong being domination by idolatrous foreign powers and the other prong being the danger of acculturation. These writers formulated their versions of the liturgical calendar to assure their communities of their places in God's purposes and to guide the communities in faithful response. Jewish liturgical life became a mark of identity: observing Sabbath and other elements of Jewish life reminded the community of who they were and how they were to live, even in challenging circumstances.

The Christian Year Developed Piece by Piece

The Christian year functioned similarly to the Jewish year: the pieces of the Christian year reinforced identity in the face of challenge. The Christian year did not come to birth as a complete liturgical calendar but developed in pieces over several centuries.

As far as we know, Jesus and his earliest followers worshiped in Jewish ways typical of their time. They likely followed the Jewish liturgical calendar.

The first distinctive liturgical element in the life of Jesus' followers was worship on the first day of the week in honor of the belief that God raised Jesus from the dead on that day (e.g. 1 Cor. 16:2; Acts 20:7). By the time of the writing of the book of Revelation (late first century CE), some communities called the first day of the week "the Lord's Day" (Rev. 1:10). From the point of view of Paul, Mark, Matthew, Luke, and other writers influenced by Jewish end-time (apocalyptic) thinking, the resurrection confirmed God's intent to end this present evil age and to replace it with the realm of God (an unending age of love, peace, joy, solidarity, and abundance).[3] The transition from the old age to the new had begun the ministry of Jesus, but the final and complete manifestation would come only with Jesus' return (the second coming, the apocalypse). Worship on the first day of the week both honored the resurrection and anticipated the second coming.[4] Worship on the first day of the week did not begin as a Christian Sabbath but functioned as an identity reminder for Jesus' followers as they lived through the brokenness of the old age.

The annual observance of Easter was the second addition to the worship calendar of the early church. Some scholars think the early church celebrated the resurrection for several weeks after Easter, a tone continuing today in the Sundays after Easter. Traditional liturgical scholarship sees Easter as an occasion for baptism.

The Day of Pentecost became the third major focal point. By the end of the second century, many churches began to honor Pentecost. The church initially celebrated ascension and Pentecost on the same day, thus reminding the church of both the sovereignty of Jesus over all earthly rulers (ascension) and the continuing presence of the Holy Spirit empowering the church to faithful life and witness (Pentecost).

The earliest evidence for Epiphany, the fourth major element of the Christian year, is in the early third century. Epiphany originally had multiple associations: Jesus' birth, the astrologers, and Jesus' baptism.

In the late third and early fourth centuries, Holy Week and then Lent became the fifth and sixth elements of the calendar. Holy Week was formed from liturgical observances of events from the last week of Jesus' life: entering Jerusalem, last supper, trial, and crucifixion. In 325 CE, the Council of Nicea spoke of forty days of preparation for Easter—the beginning of Lent. For some time Lent continued as a complex season of preparation for baptism, penitence, and reconciliation, all leading to Easter.

The Western church separated Epiphany and Christmas into distinct emphases in the early fourth century, thus making Christmas the seventh element of the Christian year. Many liturgical historians think the church chose December 25 as the date of Christmas as a polemic against (and reinterpretation of) a Roman day celebrating the birth of the sun.

Some churches added Sundays to prepare for Christmas. These Sundays eventually became Advent, the eighth major element of the Christian year. Advent was initially a time of fasting and penitence in preparation for Christmas. With respect to the liturgical calendar, the last became first; that is, the last season to develop became the first one observed in the Christian year.

The basic structure of the Christian year, then, evolved over four centuries. Some additions made their way into the subsequent calendar. All Saints, for example, was added in the ninth century, and Trinity Sunday, about 1000 CE. Over the centuries, many ecclesial movements brought their own emphases to the calendar.

The History of the Christian Year as a Resource for Preaching

While the Christian year tells a single story, the Christian year is not found as a single narrative in the Bible.[5] The church created the Christian year from bits and pieces of diverse biblical and theological materials in response to particular pastoral needs at particular moments. The Christian year and its elements are historically conditioned. The church sometimes loses sight of the created and contextual nature of the Christian year. While churches occasionally discuss amendments to the Christian year, preachers and congregations today tend to assume it without critical thought.

On the one hand, preachers who follow the Christian year could help some congregations understand the nature and function of the year by re-constructing the situations in which its parts arose and by recalling its pur-poses. The preacher might ponder resonance between the circumstances in which the church created the Christian year and circumstances today. How might the Christian year play analogous roles for the church today? On the other hand, such recovery might help a congregation recognize distance between its life and the world that gave birth to the Christian year, and to ponder alternatives to the Christian year that might better help the church today develop a robust theological consciousness and sense of mission.

The Christian Year as Theological Calendar

The Christian year presumes a particular theological interpretation of the world and God's response. The theology of the Christian year is framed by apocalyptic or end-time eschatology.[6] The present world is an evil age so broken that it cannot be fixed. God must destroy it and replace it with a new world (the realm of God). According to the Christian year, God began the transformation of the old into the new through Jesus' birth, ministry, death, and resurrection. At Jesus' return, God will complete the work of re-creating the world as a realm of love, peace, justice, solidarity, and abun-dance.[7]

The Christian year is made up of three major parts. or cycles. The first cycle begins with Advent, includes Christmas and the Sundays following, and concludes on Epiphany Day. The Advent–Christmas–Epiphany Day cycle calls attention to God's initiative through Jesus to point to the pres-ence and future of the realm of God.

The second part of the church year is the cycle that begins with Ash Wednesday, goes through Lent and Holy Week to Easter, and thence to Pentecost Day. The Lent–Easter–Pentecost Day cycle focuses attention on the death, resurrection, ascension, and return of Jesus as centerpieces in God's redeeming work, revealing the depth of opposition to God (crucifix-ion) and the superiority of God's power over all other powers (resurrection and ascension). The Holy Spirit is the ongoing agent of the Realm until Jesus returns.

The third part, Ordinary Time, refers to those parts of the year that are not included in the two great cycles of redemption. Ordinary Time occurs in segments: after Epiphany Day to Ash Wednesday, and again after Pen-tecost Day until the beginning of Advent. In Ordinary Time the church learns how to order its life in response to God's redeeming purposes.

Preachers, worship planners, and educational leaders need to explain these overarching theological motifs. While the seasons have an internal logic, their relationship may not be obvious to the parishioner who does not have an innate interest in such matters.

Brief Descriptions of the Seasons and Days

We turn now to brief descriptions of the major seasons and days of the Christian year.[8] Since references to preaching from the *Revised Common Lectionary* occur along the way, the reader needs to remember that the lectionary preacher should interpret Biblical materials from the perspective of how they help the congregation understand the theology of the season and day on which they are read.

Advent

The word *Advent* transliterates the Latin *adventus,* which means "coming." The season of Advent makes a double-edged theological point. Advent ties together the first and second comings of Jesus to stress that the redeeming work of God through Jesus that was manifest in the first advent (the birth) is not complete until the second advent (the return of Jesus). Advent is thus a time to prepare for both the first and second comings of Jesus.

Preachers may need to explain that the birth of Jesus only initiates the work of God taking place through Jesus. This is why several Gospel readings in the *Revised Common Lectionary* on the last Sundays of Ordinary Time focus on the second coming, as do the readings on the First Sunday of Advent, itself.[9] This raises the question for the preacher, "How do we prepare for this second coming?" The lectionary uses the figure of John the Baptist to represent the fundamental act of preparation: to repent from collusion with the values, practices, and powers of the idolatrous old age, and to turn toward the coming realm of God.

Only on the Fourth Sunday of Advent does the Christian year turn our attention to the birth of Jesus. The preacher could help the congregation recognize the birth of Jesus not as an end but as divine authorization of the ministry of Jesus, a work that climaxes only at the second coming.

The preacher following the *Revised Common Lectionary* may need to address a point at which some members of the church may be confused, as revealed in a parishioner's remark, "I thought Advent is the season when we anticipate the birth of the infant Jesus. Why are we talking about the second coming and John the Baptist?" The lectionary preacher needs to help the congregation toward adequate visions of Advent. The non-lectionary preacher might focus on popular associations for the four Sundays of Advent: hope, peace, joy and love, or on Christian practices that prepare the congregation for the second and first comings, such as repentance, fasting, prayer, and neighbor-love.

Christmas

Christmas Eve, Christmas Day and the Sundays after Christmas give the preacher an opportunity to explore not only the meaning of the birth of Jesus but also larger issues of Christology.[10] On a Christological spectrum, meanings of Jesus vary from the high end, which sees the birth of Jesus as the incarnation of God become flesh, to the low end, which places minimal theological significance on the birth of Jesus.

The former emphasis calls for the preacher to unpack the significance of the incarnation for the church and world. The issue for this preacher and congregation is less *how* Jesus can be both fully human and fully divine and more *why* this development matters. What does it do for church and world?

The emphasis at the other end of the Christological spectrum gives the preacher an opportunity to help the congregation think about how the birth texts can contribute to their confidence that God authorizes the ministry of Jesus. The minister can also think with the congregation about the significance of the broader ministry of Jesus in such roles as rabbi, prophet, and wisdom teacher.

Regardless of the location of the preacher on the Christological spectrum, the preacher likely faces a problem that bleeds into the church from North American Christmas culture. Many households reduce Christmas to giving and receiving gifts in a warm family time. Without disrespecting such genuine but reduced associations, the preacher needs to help the congregation open the lens of its vision to see the birth of Jesus signaling God's possibilities for renewal in a broken world.

Epiphany Day

Epiphany is not a season but a day that brings the Advent–Christmas–Epiphany cycle to a conclusion. The word *epiphany* transliterates a Greek word for "manifestation." Epiphany occurs on January 6, twelve days after Christmas. When Epiphany takes place during the week, some churches observe a Sunday near January 6 as Epiphany Sunday.

Since the *Revised Common Lectionary* assigns the same Gospel reading for Epiphany in each of the three lectionary years (Matt. 2:1-12), the visit

15

of the astrologers—gentiles whose presence in the text prefigures the gentile mission in Matthew—is the main focus of Epiphany Day. That text functions here as a theological symbol of the larger conviction that God's blessing flows through Jesus to gentiles in a way similar to its flow through Israel.

The preacher may unreflectively imply that God's love for gentiles was hidden until Jesus. To the contrary, according to the priestly theologians, the purpose of Israel's life was to model the way of blessing for gentiles (for example, Gen. 12:1-3, Isa. 42:6). Strands of the end-time thinking that influenced the Gospels and Letters looked forward to a great reunion of Jewish and gentile peoples in the Realm. The ministry of Jesus, signaling nearness of the apocalypse, points to the coming of that reunion. Jesus' followers can welcome gentiles into the eschatological community by repentance, baptism, and living in the ways of God.

Lent

Over the centuries, Lent has hosted a number of themes, including preparation for baptism, repentance, fasting, temptation, prayer, penance, almsgiving, self-denial, the passion, and now the joy of preparation for Easter. In Lent, the church names things that put us at odds with God's purposes—and that bring us into league with the powers of the old age that put Jesus to death. The church should repent of our complicity with such powers and turn toward the resources God provides for living more faithfully.

Ash Wednesday begins Lent by sounding two related notes. One is the call to remember that we are mortal. We are creatures. We are not God. Moreover, we need to face our mortality and to make the most of this mortal life, living not for ourselves but for God. The other note is the call to repent, especially of ways we have acted as if we were God and have wasted our mortality by living only for ourselves and not for God and others.

The preacher following the *Revised Common Lectionary* finds a number of provocative biblical passages in Lent that have unusual force in shaping Christian consciousness, such as Jesus' encounter with Nicodemus (John 3:1-17), Jesus and the woman at the well (John 4:5-42), the parable of the parent and the two heirs (Luke 15:11b-32). Yet a preacher's responsibility is to develop sermons that specifically serve Lent. When preaching on such texts, the preacher needs to take larger Lenten concerns into consideration. Unfortunately, while the lectionary intends for Lent to prepare the congregation for the joy of Easter, the Lenten texts do not build on one another across the five Sundays of Lenten preaching.

A non-lectionary preacher sometimes has a Lenten advantage over the lectionary preacher in that the non-lectionary preacher may more easily put together sermons dealing with foundational Lenten themes with thematic continuity from Sunday to Sunday.

The church today encounters a challenge in Holy Week. In earlier times, congregations recalled Jesus' entry into Jerusalem on Palm Sunday, walked with Jesus to the Last Supper, stood on Golgotha on Good Friday, and waited through Holy Saturday for the Easter vigil. This pattern has gone awry since contemporary congregations have few Holy Week services, and the services that congregations sponsor are poorly attended. In congregations that go directly from Palm Sunday to Easter, members do not face Jesus' death at the hands of the old age. The congregation goes from an up, Palm Sunday, to an upper up, Easter.

Consequently, a lot of congregations have converted Palm Sunday into Palm/Passion Sunday through a service that begins with the entry into Jerusalem but moves to the events leading to the cross. When the preacher accompanies this service with significant interpretation, such a service can be compelling, especially with respect to our own collusion with the brokenness of the old world. However, some congregations simply read the passion story without commentary. A problem in this approach is that the stories of the death of Jesus in all four Gospels are shot through with negative caricatures of Jewish leaders. When these caricatures are unchallenged, as when they are simply read aloud, they can contribute to anti-Judaism and anti-Semitism. A preacher should always call attention to such distortions in the passion story.

The meaning of the death of Jesus is debated today. At one end of the interpretive spectrum is Jesus' death as substitutionary atonement while at the other end is Jesus' death as martyrdom at the hands of the old age. A popular proverb summarizes the latter: Jesus did not die for our sin but because of our sin. Passion Sunday and Good Friday invite sermons that help the congregation wrestle with the cross.

Lent in early twenty-first-century congregations may be a good time to recover the historic emphasis on preparation for baptism. Many participants in church today struggle with Christian identity. Baptism is to assure the baptisands of Christian identity and to direct them toward mission. For the non-lectionary preacher, Lent could be an ideal time for a sermon series on baptism, especially its contribution to Christian identity and the ways it impels us to mission.

17

Easter

The season of Easter begins on Easter Day with the resurrection, the pivotal event of the Christian story. From end-time perspective, the resurrection is the definitive sign that the old age is passing away and the new world is coming. Moreover, the resurrection embodies the qualities of life of the new world. From Johannine perspective, the resurrection shows that all who believe in Jesus can experience heaven (light, truth, freedom, peace, abundance, and everlasting life with God above) within the present (with its darkness, lying, slavery, violence, scarcity, and death). Both schools of thought stress a common note: despite the pervasiveness of death, the power of God—the power of life—prevails. The preacher's job is to help people identify the presence of that power, trust it, and act in conjunction with it.

The Sundays after Easter draw out the implications of the resurrection. The RCL opens the way for an important emphasis on these Sundays. While some of the Gospel readings focus directly on the resurrection, many do not. The preacher can then help the congregation recognize that all the Gospels have the risen Jesus in view: the power at work described in the ministry of Jesus in the Gospels continues to be at work through the resurrected Jesus in the church.

Ministers sometimes misrepresent Easter in two ways. First, some preachers treat Easter as if it is the climax of the Christian story. From a theological point of view, the second coming is that climax. Second, Easter sermons sometimes speak as if the goal of the resurrection is to open the way to eternal life for believers. As noted previously, the resurrection of Jesus points not only to the resurrection of the faithful but also to the reconstitution of the cosmos.

Pentecost Day

Pentecost Day brings the Easter cycle to a climax by connecting the resurrection to the Spirit. Through the Spirit, the same power that operated in Jesus is still at work in the church. Pentecost thus points forward to Ordinary Time: since the Spirit continues to work in the church, the church can minister in the same ways that the Gospels picture Jesus ministering in Ordinary Time.

In the Gospels and Letters, the name "Pentecost" occurs only in connection with Acts 2:1-42. To be sure, John 20:19-23 contains a version of Jesus giving the Spirit to the disciples, and the Spirit figures prominently in many other passages in the Gospels and Letters. Yet the emphasis on the Spirit in Acts plays a large hand in the church's theological consciousness of Pentecost Day. For Luke, on Pentecost God poured out an extra measure of the Spirit to empower the church during the tensions of the last days (Acts 2:17). The Spirit sustains the church and empowers its witness during conflicts while the church awaits the second coming. Welcoming gentiles is a central feature of this witness. Indeed, the gentile mission is part of the eschatological harvest taking place at the transition of the ages.

A preacher should alert the congregation to the diversity of interpretations of the Spirit not only in the Gospels and Letters but in the rest of the Bible and in Christian history. A lectionary preacher might compare and contrast other understandings of the Spirit with those found in the Pentecost readings. Pentecost Day is the perfect entry point for a non-lectionary minister to pursue the doctrine of the Holy Spirit.

For both lectionary and non-lectionary preachers, Pentecost Day provides a natural agenda for discussing the relationship between more and less ecstatic expressions of the Spirit in the church today. A preacher might further explore how the Spirit is active in the world outside Judaism and the church.

Preachers sometimes make an exegetical and theological mistake with respect to Pentecost by claiming that at the time of Luke, the Jewish community believed the Spirit was not active in the world. From this perspective the story of Pentecost tells of God returning the Spirit. To the contrary, the core of the Jewish community always believed the Spirit was active (e.g. 1QS 3:6; 9:3-6; Wisd. Sol. 1:6-7; 12:1; 2 Esd. 14:22). For Luke-Acts the outpouring of the Spirit on Pentecost was a sign that the last days were at hand.

Ordinary Time

Christians sometimes dismiss Ordinary Time as unimportant. As my spouse says, "No one likes to think they are ordinary." However, the etymology of the word *ordinary* suggests the meaning of this time. The word comes from the Latin *ordinalis,* which refers to numbers in a sequence. *Ordinalis,* in turn, is related to *ordo,* which refers to order. The Sundays in Ordinary Time are numbered, as in Second Sunday after the Epiphany or Proper 26. The numbers are not important in themselves, but they softly point to the purpose of the season: to help the church learn how to order its life in response to God's ministry through Jesus. Ordinary Time helps the congregation increase its awareness of what God offers by way of love, grace, peace, justice, community, and abundance, and to respond appropriately.

19

For Ordinary Time the preacher might turn to sermons that help the congregation grow in discipleship. A minister could preach through a book of the Bible, do a series on biblical texts or themes, or speak about Christian doctrine or Christian practice.

A preacher following the *Revised Common Lectionary* asks of the assigned readings, "How does conversation with these passages help the congregation grow in discipleship?" On the Sundays in Ordinary Time after Epiphany Day, the Gospel readings move from the baptism of Jesus through the beginning of Jesus' ministry, thus giving the preacher the opportunity to help the congregation reflect on the role baptism plays in the life of the community and on essential themes of Jesus' ministry and of the life of discipleship. For example, this season gives us the Sermon on the Mount (Matt. 5–7) and the Sermon the Plain (Luke 6:17-49).

In Ordinary Time from the Sunday after Pentecost Day to the beginning of Advent, the lectionary offers possibilities for preaching through major parts of the Gospels and Letters, as well as preaching through segments of the Torah, Prophets, and Writings. The preacher must figure out which approach is most generative for nurturing the congregation at the time of preaching.

Strengths of the Christian Year

A number of preachers and scholars of preaching envision the Christian year as the only context for preaching. "I can't imagine beginning anywhere else," a minister said to me during a conversation about this book. Indeed the Christian year has significant strengths as a starting point for preaching. Several of these strengths, like several weaknesses, intersect with strong and weak points of the RCL. I try to keep repetition to a minimum between this chapter and the following two chapters on the *Revised Common Lectionary*, but a certain amount of overlap creeps in.

Keeps Big Themes of Christian Theology in Congregational Consciousness

The themes of the Christian year include some foundational notions for Christian theology, identity, and mission. The heart of the Christian year is the story of God taking the initiative to act in love through Jesus for the sake of the broken world. The Christian year keeps before us the appropriate responses to God's action: trusting in what God has done, is doing, and will do, and living in ways consistent with God's purposes. As we saw in the short descriptions of the Seasons and Days in the previous section, the seasons of the Christian year illumine different nuances of God's work through Jesus.

Preachers and worship planners left to themselves to select foci for worship often succumb (perhaps unconsciously) to one or more of several distortions. Many congregations have theological amnesia. They forget the depth of what God does and what we are to do in response. Preachers often ride hobby horses in choosing biblical texts and theological themes. Preachers can assimilate so many values and behaviors from the culture that the sermon becomes little more than a celebration of the culture, with its brokenness, compromise, and idolatry. Preachers can sometimes be mesmerized by immediate situations and can forget to look toward larger theological visions. Preachers can hide from challenging theological notions. The themes in the Christian year call preachers and congregations to keep the big theological picture in mind.

The Themes of the Year Become Engrained over Time

We learn to play the piano by practice. With enough good-quality practice, moving our fingers on the piano becomes instinctive. With the right kind and amount of practice, we soon do not have to think consciously about how to move our fingers because such movements are engrained. However, if we do not continue to practice, the instincts to play often diminish; our fingers move more slowly and are less familiar with the keyboard. Continued practice is necessary to maintain peak ability.

Similarly, many theologians hold that doing something over and over in the life of the church encourages that thing to become engrained in the mind, heart, and behavior of Christian community.[11] The seasons of the Christian year bring foundational matters before the congregation, especially with respect to the brokenness of the world, God's redemptive initiative through Christ, and our response. Observing the Christian year helps initiate newcomers into the core of Christian community while helping the rest of the congregation keep in practice.

Having the themes of the Christian year engrained does not mean that the church can shut off thinking. The Christian year intends for patterns of Christian thought and behavior to become second nature so that, in many situations, Christians do not have to pause and think about how to interpret or how to act. Like the first responders on the scene of a trauma, the church just knows what to do. In other situations, when the church does need to pause and think, it has in place some resources for doing so.[12]

The church does need to reflect critically on the theological quality of its observance of the Christian year. Simply observing the Christian year does not guarantee that a congregation will get and stay in practice. When playing the piano, we can get into bad habits and may need to relearn how to play at a good level. The church, likewise, can misperceive or misuse the Christian year and sometimes needs to reform its practice.

Intends for Worship to Include Both Word and Table

The liturgical reform following Vatican II envisions the fullness of Christian worship including both word and table. This movement began in the Roman Catholic Church, in which worship climaxes in the Sacred Meal. From the Roman Catholic side, renewal of worship includes reemphasizing the act of preaching as a means through which Jesus becomes present in the community. On the Protestant side, renewal includes reemphasizing the Sacred Meal as an essential constituent part of weekly worship.

Today, most theologians of worship think of worship as an ellipsis—a closed arc with two foci: the sermon and the Sacred Meal. Preaching not only explicitly interprets God's presence and leading but is an experience of grace. The Sacred Meal is a visible sign that God uses to assure the congregation of the divine presence and leading. When the congregation eats the bread and drinks the cup, the community commits itself to living in God's ways.

Although almost fifty years have passed since the beginning of the liturgical reform, few Protestant congregations partake of the Sacred Meal every week. However, the Christian year implicitly keeps that meal before the congregation. As a lifelong member of the Christian Church (Disciples of Christ), a movement that has practiced weekly communion since its beginning, I testify that keeping the Feast every Sunday does not cheapen the experience. On the contrary, in the best sense of Christian practice, the weekly experience of receiving loaf and cup deepens a community's awareness of the immediate, unconditional, and empowering presence of the living God.

Emphasizes Assurance of God's Presence and Activity While Inviting Faithful Response

The Christian year embodies good theology by placing the indicative and the imperative in proper theological relationship: God's action and our response. To oversimplify, the two major cycles of the Christian year— Advent–Christmas–Epiphany Day, and Lent–Easter–Pentecost Day— emphasize God's redemptive presence and activity; Ordinary Time emphasizes our response. Of course, the two great cycles presume our response, and Ordinary Time presumes God's constant work for the world. But for heuristic purposes, we can note that the year begins with *God's* initiative while calling for *our responses* of trust and witness.

This approach has a double strength. First, the Christian year answers the two fundamental questions of life for every individual and community. (1) Who are we? We are a community beloved by God. The unconditional love of God is the ground of our existence, our self-understanding, and our understanding of others, and the world. (2) What are we to do? We are to love one another as God loves us.

Second, the Christian year works against persistent human effort to justify ourselves by works. Although people these days do not often use the language of works righteousness, the human attempt to justify our own worth through what we do is commonplace. For those who never do enough to feel worthy, the Christian year comes as welcome relief: "*You* do not have to do things to justify your worth. *God* has already done that for you." For those who think their accomplishments have satisfied their deepest longings and desires, the Christian year is a reminder: No matter what *you* do, you cannot ultimately save yourself. If you believe in what God has done, is doing, and will do, you will experience unimagined depths of life, love, and purpose.

Reminds the Church That God Promises More in Life

The Christian calendar is out of sync with the other calendars in early twenty-first-century North America. The Christian year begins in late November or early December with the First Sunday of Advent and ends in late November with the Sunday known as Reign of Christ, or Christ the Cosmic Ruler. By contrast, the basic secular calendar year begins January 1 and ends December 31. Fiscal years sometimes begin July 1 and end June 30. The traditional school year began in late August or early September and ended in late May or early June. Schools in year-round session now start and stop at different times throughout the year. The major holidays of the civic calendar—Martin Luther King Jr. Day, President's Day, Memorial Day, Fourth of July, Labor Day, Thanksgiving Day—do not correspond to traditional Christian days. In the secular world, Christmas is a commercial season. For some congregations, the program year—youth programming, small group Bible studies, and so on—is from early October through the end of April.

The incompatibility of the Christian year with other calendars makes an important point: Christians live with a worldview determined by God's gracious activity that differs from secular calendars or worldviews. From the perspective of end-time theology, secular calendars often perpetuate values and behaviors that belong to the old age, whereas the church lives according to a calendar with redemption as its goal.

Adequate preaching and teaching can help the congregation realize that living according to a different calendar means living with a different world-view from secular society. The church is tempted to think that the broken world is pretty much life as it can be. The annual cycle in the Christian year reminds the church not to settle for this depressing situation. Indeed, the Christian calendar points to God's promise of a renewed world now and forever. Of course, the year reminds us that we need to do our part through repentance and through living toward that world.

Symbolizes the Unity of the Church

Participating in the Christian year symbolizes the church as true community, the inherent relatedness not only of Christians within congregations, but also of congregations with other congregations in the church universal. Inherent relationship, in this case, refers neither to institutional nor theological uniformity but to the baptismal fact that all Christians and churches are related to one another. However, this is a unity-with-diversity. As a student commented, "We are related with one another whether we know it or not, and whether we like it or not." While the church contains many differences, these differences are not all divisive and fractious. Indeed, many differences enrich the church's diverse theologies and witness.

Some differences, however, are major, even contradictory. While not all churches observe the Christian year, observing the Christian year implies not only a sense of relationship to the larger church but also a willingness to explore with other churches how to interpret Christian theology and witness today. At times, such interaction may lead churches to engage in common belief and witness. At other times, conversation may lead the church to recognize that common belief and witness is not possible. At such times, the church can model respect-amidst-disagreement. The capacity to maintain relationship and respect in the midst of disagreement might be one of the church's best gifts to the fractious culture of the early twenty-first century.

The Christian year can become the basis of cooperative events among Christians, especially among clergy of different congregations and denominations. Advent workshops, for instance, can involve preachers and congregations from across the denominational spectrum. Such ecumenical-interdenominational efforts can have the effect of cross-pollination. Such efforts are good stewardship by making optimum use of limited resources. Moreover, when members of different congregations encounter one another in nonchurch settings—such as workplaces, restaurants, community service projects, recreation facilities, and athletic events—they sometimes talk about what happened in their respective congregations on recent Sundays.

Pushes the Preacher to Consider Ideas the Preacher Might Avoid

As noted earlier, preachers and worship planners sometimes have their own hobby horses in the way of biblical texts, theological themes, Christian practices, pastoral issues, and ethical perspectives to which they turn again and again. Consciously or unconsciously, preachers and worship planners often avoid certain texts, themes, practices, issues, and ethical matters. The Christian year pushes the preacher to consider a broad range of theological ideas, including some that the preacher would prefer to ignore.

For example, growing up in a congregation emphasizing (1) that rational study of the Bible and Christian doctrine could lead one to confidence in God and (2) that such confidence was grounded in God's promise and action and not in my own experience, I had little interest in the Holy Spirit. Indeed, my distant disdain for the emotionally demonstrative experience of the Spirit in the Pentecostal churches only reinforced my lack of interest in the Spirit. The Christian year, however, pushes the church to think about the Holy Spirit on Pentecost Day.

Accommodates Different Theological Families

On the one hand, as noted previously, the Christian year presupposes an overarching end-time theological framework. On the other, preachers can interpret the end-time theology of the Christian year from the perspectives of their own specific theological families, especially regarding the *specific content* of redemption, *how* God operates, and how theological content relates to particular issues, social circumstances, and philosophical and scientific perspectives in the contemporary world.

The Christian year can thus accommodate different theological families. Preachers interpret themes of the Christian year through the perspectives of their particular theologies. Indeed, we may identify at least ten distinct theological families in North America today: liberal theology, mutual critical correlation, process theology, fundamentalism, evangelical theology, postliberalism, neo-orthodox, theologies of otherness, liberation theologies,

25

and ethnic theologies.[13] Each family (and theologians within them) puts forward distinct perspectives on God, Jesus, the Holy Spirit, the church, the world, God's immediate and ultimate purposes, and how the church and the world can participate with these purposes. At the beginning of Advent, for instance, a minister does not simply preach about the second coming but develops a sermon from the perspective of how the preacher's theological family interprets the second coming.

Helps with Planning

The Christian year and the *Revised Common Lectionary* give preachers (and worship leaders) a place to start planning for individual services and seasons of worship. Ministers do not have to start from scratch each Monday, wondering, "Where am I going to get a sermon this week?" The season gives the preacher a field of theological focus. The particular Sunday may sharpen this focus even more. If the preacher follows the lectionary, the preacher begins the conversation leading to the sermon with the lectionary readings. Beginning sermon preparation from the Christian year means that preachers can make fruitful use of their limited time for sermon preparation.

Adds Variety to Worship

Each season of the Christian year has its own theological emphases, psychological dynamics, liturgical traditions, and colors. These things add variety to preaching and worship. The church should not play into the addiction to the new and different that troubles Eurocentric North American culture, and should try to avoid that culture's entertainment syndrome. Nevertheless, variety is a spice in life. Change can cause us to sit up and take notice. When the variety and change of the Christian year are managed in a theologically healthy way, they can help keep the congregation engaged.

Weaknesses of the Christian Year

After considering the strengths of the Christian year, the reader may think, "There is so much here, why consider other options?" Yet, the strengths of the Christian year cannot mask its weaknesses. With respect to preaching, some of these dangers are more in how preachers handle these themes than they are in the themes themselves, but some are inherent in the Christian year.

Neglects God's Activity Prior to Jesus

The Christian year neglects God's activity prior to Jesus. Indeed, the Christian year focuses entirely on the story of Jesus: the Christian year begins with the expectation of Jesus' return and then moves through Jesus' birth, teaching, passion, resurrection, and ascension; the outpouring of the Spirit; and Jesus' return. A congregation following the Christian year alone—without the *Revised Common Lectionary*—might never encounter the story of Israel.[14] Indeed, based on the Christian year alone, one could get the impression that nothing of theological importance happened before Jesus, and that God is ultimately concerned only about those who are redeemed through Jesus.

When the *Revised Common Lectionary* is nested within the Christian year, the lectionary does bring the story of God's activity in Israel directly into the consciousness of the congregation. However, as chapter 3 of this book will point out, the *Revised Common Lectionary* actually intensifies aspects of this problem.

For two reasons, neglecting God's presence and purposes in Israel is a significant theological mistake. First, the ministry of Jesus can only be understood in the network of themes, events, and characters in the history, theology, and literature of Israel. The writers of the Gospels and Letters use primarily Jewish categories to interpret the ministry of Jesus. Jesus' own teaching and activities are Jewish in origin and character. Indeed, the end-time hope is a Jewish hope. Without immersion in the stories of Israel, preacher and congregation cannot adequately understand Jesus and the church.

Second, the work of God through Jesus is part of the story of Israel. The ministry of Jesus and the church do not negate or replace God's witness through Israel. According to writers of the Gospels and Letters influenced by end-time theology, the ministry of Jesus and the church have two distinct elements. First, the ministry of Jesus is a signal that the end-times are at hand, when God will fulfill the promises God made to Israel by finally and fully manifesting the divine Realm. Second, in view of the impending apocalypse, gentiles are now welcome in the eschatological community (the church) awaiting the apocalypse.

The structure of the Christian year does not specifically call attention to the story of Jesus as a Jewish story. Unless the preacher does so, the congregation may miss these connections.

Moreover, when the story of Israel is implied in the Christian year, the implications often cast Jewish people in a negative light. Advent, for instance, implies that the people of Israel are theologically unfulfilled. This aspect of the Advent mood is captured in the opening line of a beloved Advent hymn: "O come, O come, Emmanuel, and ransom captive Israel, that mourns in lowly exile here, until the Son of God appear."[15] In this hymn, the Jewish people are only in a state of longing. In Holy Week, the Jewish leadership and the Jewish crowd are typically pictured as instrumental in the death of Jesus. Christian narrations of Pentecost sometimes imply that the Spirit was not active in the world until Jesus.

Christians sometimes speak as if the world contained no real hope or love prior to Jesus. At Christmas, for instance, preachers sometimes say that love was born at Bethlehem. Christians sometimes claim that Jesus and the church replaced or superseded Judaism. Although the Bible never refers to the church as "the new Israel," Christians sometimes do, thus implying that the old Israel is worn out and has been replaced.

Whether or not the framers of the Christian year intended these effects, the Christian year can contribute to anti-Judaism and anti-Semitism. Preachers who follow the Christian year in its present form need to warn congregations against the anti-Jewish distortions that can creep into the Christian year, and to encourage congregations toward respect for Jewish people and mutual witness to the living God. Beyond that, I believe the church should rethink the structure of the Christian year to bring the story of Israel into the consciousness of the church in a healthy theological way.

Overlooks Some Important Theological Themes

The preceding section commends the broad expanse of motifs in the Christian year. Indeed, the themes of the Christian year sometimes push the preacher to consider theological ideas that are outside the preacher's comfort zone. However, at the same time, the Christian year does bring some important theological perspectives into the congregation.

For example, users of the Christian year usually focus on the redemption of human beings. The Christian year gives no direct attention to the created world as such. Indeed, the end-time theology in back of the Christian year envisions God replacing the present natural world with a new earth and a new heaven. When ecocide is a possibility, such neglect is regrettable. More than fifty years ago, A. A. McArthur proposed a season of creation, but churches did not find it compelling.[16] Recently, aware of the increasing tensions between humankind and nature, and mindful of the solidarity that should exist between these two, a fresh approach calls for four Sundays each year as a season of creation. The creators envision the season being observed between September 1 and St. Francis Day (October 4) or at other appropriate times of the year. The readings in Year A focus on the Spirit and creation, in Year B on the word and creation, and in Year C on wisdom and creation.[17]

To cite another example, Timothy Slemmons proposes a "principle of canonical comprehensiveness" to foster representation of a wider selection of biblical material in the lectionary.[18] Slemmons thus formulates Year D, a fourth year to add to the current lectionary. Year D is largely made up of readings not found in the current lectionary. The readings tend to be longer than in the *Revised Common Lectionary*, to lean more toward continuous reading, and to give greater emphasis to the Torah, Prophets, and Writings. In the major seasons, the texts in Year D look at the themes of the days from fresh angles. Ordinary time contains extensive readings from Jesus' apocalyptic discourse, from the prelude to the passion, and from the passion.[19]

We could point to many other theological lacunas. For example while the Christian year highlights the work of God through Christ, it gives little direct attention to the notions of revelation (how we come to interpret God's purposes), providence, or evil. The year never specifically focuses on mission or justice.[20] Particular denominations and Christian movements may find that the Christian year does not adequately offer theological resources for themes central to their theology and practice.

Controlled by End-Time Theology

The Christian year is controlled by end-time (apocalyptic) theology. The first Sunday of Advent begins the Christian year with a focus on the second coming of Jesus. Each year, the lectionary designates a Gospel reading from an apocalyptic discourse from a synoptic Gospel for the First Sunday in Advent. The last Sundays of the Christian year move toward Christ the Cosmic Ruler with lectionary texts pointing toward the apocalypse.[21] A leading purpose of the Christian year is to prepare the congregation for the second coming.

The apocalyptic theology of the Gospels and Letters does contain a present element—the ministry of Jesus begins to manifest elements of the realm of God in the present, and the life of the church continues to embody many of those elements—but God's purposes will be fully and finally fulfilled only after the apocalypse.

The apocalyptic nature of the Christian year raises two issues for the church today. First, apocalypticism is only one of the diverse theologies in the Bible. The apocalyptic worldview does permeate the synoptic Gospels, the letters of Paul and those who wrote in his name, several other letters, and the book of Revelation. But a more realized eschatology is found in the Gospel and Letters of John. We find fully developed apocalyptic theology in only six chapters of the Torah, Prophets, and Writings (Dan. 7–12). The other theological families in the Torah, Prophets, and Writings envision God's purposes becoming manifest in present world history largely through historical process. The canon thus does not itself make end-time theology normative.

Second, a good many Christians today do not believe the end-time worldview. That is, they do not believe that history is divided into two distinct ages and that we await a cosmic second coming. The reasons for such skepticism are both theological and scientific. It is logically incoherent to believe that God is unconditional love and has the power to end suffering in a single stroke but allows suffering to continue generation after generation. Continuing in such a hope makes little sense when we have waited for an apocalypse for two thousand years and there are still no indications it is likely to happen. In fact, the actual conditions of life among humankind and nature are no better than they were at the time of the Gospels and Letters. In the face of such issues, some Christians turn to other theological families to interpret God's ultimate presence and leading.[22]

One of the purposes of preaching is to help congregations makes sense of Christian tradition for the contemporary context. This task includes interpreting the apocalyptic hope for today. Indeed, as is noted in connection with the strengths mentioned earlier, the Christian year can accommodate diverse theological viewpoints. Some contemporary expressions of eschatology are theologically appropriate and believable, but the apocalyptic overlay of the Christian year can make them hard to see and access.

Can Become Anesthetic Due to Repetition

On the one hand, observing the Christian year over and over and over again can help the church become intuitively familiar. On the other hand, such repetition can become anesthetic. Familiarity can turn to lack of attentiveness. Preacher and congregation can pass through the Christian year assuming, unreflectively, that they already know what they need to know about the seasons of the Christian year and about how these interact with their immediate context in life. Even worse, preacher and congregation can be bored by the repetition of the year. At the beginning of Advent, a comrade parishioner sighed, "Here we go again," as if to say, "We've been here so many times before."

Preaching from different lectionary texts brings a measure of variety to congregations that follow the lectionary. However, the next chapter notes that the diversity within the lectionary is itself limited.

Repetition drifting into boredom is not inherent in the Christian year.

Indeed, a part of the preacher's calling is to find life-giving connections between the Christian year and the situation of the congregation. In the search for freshness, however, preachers need to guard against developing an ecclesial entertainment mentality.

Themes May Not Fit the Preaching Context

A foundational calling of the preacher is to bring a life-giving word through conversation with the Bible and/or Christian theology to the congregation. Preachers sometimes marvel at the fit between the Christian year and the life of the community. The Ash Wednesday call to repent, for instance, may correlate almost perfectly with the discovery that the congregation is spending its budget for its own comfort when people are hungry just a few blocks from the church building.

Preachers can often make a bridge between emphases of the Christian year and the situation of the congregation even when a connection is not obvious. For example, while a congregation suffering from a natural disaster needs a word of comfort, the Ash Wednesday call to repent may be appropriate by helping the congregation turn away from superficial values, behaviors, and investments that preceded the disaster and to rebuild its life in ways that are more consistent with its deepest values.

However, the themes of the Christian year do not always correlate with the circumstances of the congregation. The Ash Wednesday call to repent may not fit the moment when an elderly couple in the congregation is killed when their pickup truck collides with a semi-tractor trailer truck on a county road. While a preacher might be able to build a bridge from the Christian year to the congregation when connections are not obvious, the preacher might spend so much time building the bridge that the preacher has little time to help the congregation find its way. God's immediate purposes might better be served by preaching that is not constrained by the Christian year.

Tends toward Legalism and Even Idolatry

Some preachers exhibit a tendency toward legalism of the Christian year. With respect to the Christian year, legalists act as if the Christian year is *necessary* for a congregation to have proper exposure to the great themes of the Christian faith. Preachers who act as if the Christian year is the only pattern for preaching and worship in the congregation take a dangerous step toward making an idol of the Christian year. Few ministers are openly legalistic with respect to the Christian year. Few ministers would say that a congregation can understand God only within the Christian year. But a legalistic spirit can creep into a minister's attitude.

Ministers and congregations may find it helpful to remember that the Christian year is intended to serve the purposes of God. The congregation is not intended to serve the Christian year. When observing the Christian year becomes stiff or wooden, a preacher might consider alternative starting points for preaching or try revitalizing the starting points within the Christian year.

While the Christian year has much to commend it as a starting point for preaching, it is not a perfect instrument. In my view, while it might help the congregation toward a meaningful interpretation of God's presence and purposes, it does not always do so. The preacher needs to make a judgment as to when to follow the Christian year and when to go another way.

CHAPTER 2

Preaching from the *Revised Common Lectionary*: Strengths

I imagine most preachers have had experiences similar to mine with the *Revised Common Lectionary*. I have been through seasons and years when I preached only from the lectionary and through seasons and years when I have not preached from the lectionary at all. I have been a member of congregations in which ministers preached only from the lectionary, and those in which ministers preached from the lectionary only occasionally or never at all.

At times, as both preacher and listener, the RCL seems to fit hand in glove with the moment. Indeed, as someone quoted in the introduction to this book said, "I can't believe how texts in the lectionary match up so well with the situation in our congregation right now." At other times, the lectionary passages might have been assigned for another planet. I have been sympathetic with another preacher quoted in the introduction, "I don't know why a preacher would ever become a prisoner of the lectionary."

This chapter explores the *Revised Common Lectionary* as a starting point for preparing the sermon. We look at the history of lectionaries and at how the RCL works and then identify strengths of the RCL. The next chapter considers weaknesses of that lectionary.

As noted earlier, in my view, a sermon should help a congregation come to an adequate interpretation of the presence and purposes of God, and to an appropriate response. The preacher must decide whether starting from the *Revised Common Lectionary* or from another source gives the congregation an optimum opportunity to come to such interpretations both for one Sunday and over a long period of time.

What Is a Lectionary?

The word *lectionary* comes from the Latin *lectio* meaning "reading." A lectionary is a systematic sequence of passages from the Bible assigned for reading in public worship. The individual scripture passages are sometimes called "lections," and the collection of scripture passages in a lectionary is sometimes called a "table of readings." Over the centuries the church has generated many different lectionaries. A minister following a lectionary preaches from one or more lections.

There are two kinds of lectionaries. (1) *Lectio selecta* refers to "selected readings" in which, from Sunday to Sunday, the church selects passages from different parts of the Bible to read on specific days of the Christian year. (2) *Lectio continua* refers to "continuous reading" in which the church reads continuously through parts of the Bible. For example, the church might read through the book of Romans.

A Brief History of the Lectionary

Preachers sometimes think that reading from the Bible has always been part of worship.[1] To tell the truth, we do not know precisely when Jewish communities began to read sacred texts in public worship. By the exile or shortly thereafter, the Deuteronomistic and priestly theologians seem to presume such a practice (Deut. 31:10-12; 2 Kgs. 22:8-13; 23:1-3; 2 Chr. 34:29-33). Nehemiah gives the fullest picture of a public reading from Torah followed by an exposition (Neh. 7:53b–8:8). By the time of Jesus, reading from the Torah and Prophets was evidently an established part of worship (for example, Luke 4:16-30; Acts 13:13-16, 26-38; 15:21; 1 Tim. 4:13).[2] Justin Martyr (100–165 CE) indicates that readings from the prophets and "the memoirs of the apostles" were read in worship in his part of the ecclesial world.[3]

While reading from sacred tradition may have been a regular part of the synagogue by the time of Jesus, we do not know for sure when the Jewish community began to use lectionaries. Many scholars think Luke presumes the existence of a lectionary when picturing Jesus reading from Isaiah in Luke 4:16-20, and again when depicting worship in the synagogue at Antioch of Pisidia (Acts 13:14, 27). While some scholars have attempted to reconstruct lectionaries in the synagogue from the first century, we do not have certain evidence of a table of readings.[4]

It seems the church had no golden period of lectionary origin. After lectionaries became a part of Christian practice, churches varied in the number of readings assigned for each Sunday, in the passages read, and in the relationship between selected readings and the days and seasons. Alcuin

(732–804 CE), a noted educator and liturgical reformer, brought some order to the lectionary, even while location variations persisted.

We have a clearer window into the development of lectionaries in connection with the Reformation. The Lutheran and Anglican churches formulated lectionaries largely based on Alcuin's assignments. The Reformed churches were mixed, sometimes following lectionary practice and sometimes not. The radical Reformation generally eschewed lectionaries. For its part, the Roman Catholic Council of Trent affirmed an official lectionary (1507).

In North America, the Roman Catholic, Episcopal, and Lutheran churches have long followed lectionaries. Reformed churches have been mixed in their lectionary use. As noted in the introduction, preachers in many other historic churches often freely chose their own preaching texts or topics through the late twentieth century. However, the Second Vatican Council set in motion a pattern of liturgical reform that was taken up by many historic Protestant churches. This reform reclaimed the Christian year as the framework for worship and incorporated lectionary readings into worship. The *Revised Common Lectionary* emerged from this process as the most commonly used lectionary, adjusted in minor ways for denominational preferences.

Like the Christian year, the RCL did not drop out of heaven but was created by the church. In response to changing perceptions of the needs of the church, church leaders have modified lectionaries over the centuries. Indeed, discussion about lectionary reform continues.

How the Lectionary Works

The *Revised Common Lectionary* is a three-year lectionary that appoints readings from the Bible for each Sunday of the Christian year (and some other days as well): a Gospel; a letter; a reading or readings from the Torah, Prophets and Writings, and a psalm.[5] The psalm is intended more for liturgical use than for preaching, but preachers sometimes find the psalm to be a good starting point for the sermon. The lectionary refers to the three years by nontheological names: Year A, Year B, and Year C.

The Bible Readings in Relationship to the Seasons

With respect to the relationship of the Bible readings to the seasons and days for which they are appointed, the *Revised Common Lectionary* is a *selected* lectionary for the cycles of Advent–Christmas–Epiphany Day and Lent–Easter–Pentecost Day. On the Sundays after Easter, the lectionary retains the psalm, but replaces the reading from the Torah, Prophets, and Writings with a passage from Acts.

In both sections of Ordinary Time (after Epiphany Day and after Pentecost Day), the RCL shifts to *semi-continuous* readings of the Gospels as well as *semi-continuous* readings of the Letters. These readings for Ordinary Time are chosen to promote growth in discipleship. In Ordinary Time after Pentecost Day, the lectionary provides two sets of readings from the Torah, Prophets, and Writings: one set that is semi-continuous and one set that coordinates with the Gospel. The following table represents this distribution.

Advent–Christmas–Epiphany Day	Ordinary Time after Epiphany Day	Lent–Easter–Pentecost Day	Sundays after Easter	Pentecost Day	Ordinary Time after Pentecost Day
Gospel (selected)	Gospel (semi-continuous)	Gospel (selected)	Gospel (selected)	Gospel (selected)	Gospel (semi-continuous)
Letter (selected)	Letter (semi-continuous)	Letter (selected)	Letter (selected)	Letter (selected)	Letter (semi-continuous)
			Acts		
Torah, Prophets, and Writings (selected)	Torah, Prophets, and Writings (selected)	Torah, Prophets, and Writings (selected)		Torah, Prophets, and Writings (selected)	Torah, Prophets, and Writings (selected)
Psalm	Psalm	Psalm	Psalm	Psalm	
					Torah, Prophets, and Writings (semi-continuous)
					Psalm

The Bible Readings in Relationship to One Another on a Given Sunday

As noted, with respect to the relationship of the Bible readings within each day, the *Revised Common Lectionary* puts forward different patterns.[6] During Advent–Christmas–Epiphany Day and Lent–Easter–Pentecost Day, the lectionary appoints just one set of readings: All four lessons theoretically cohere around a theological theme important to the day. The Gospel takes the lead, with the other readings in support. The preacher interprets these texts through themes of the seasons.

During Ordinary Time after Pentecost Day, the RCL appoints the same Gospel lesson and the same epistle lesson for every Sunday. The letters are read continuously or semi-continuously. The letters do not coordinate with the Gospel. In addition, the lectionary sets out two different possibilities for the psalm and the lesson from the Torah, Prophets, and Writings. The preacher and worship planners must choose which set to follow. One reading from the Torah, Prophets, and Writings and one psalm *coordinate* with the Gospel. This arrangement is often called "paired readings." Another reading from the Torah, Prophets, and Writings and psalm are semi-continuous and *do not coordinate* with the Gospel. The aim of this latter mode is to introduce the congregation to significant stories and themes in the Torah, Prophets, and Writings.

Relationship of the Paired Reading from the Torah, Prophets, and Writings to the Gospel

As noted, during Advent–Christmas–Epiphany Day and Lent–Easter–Pentecost Day, a reading from the Torah, Prophets, and Writings and a psalm is coordinated with the reading from the Gospel. During Ordinary Time, the lectionary provides one such set of four readings. On these Sundays, the lectionary committee intends that the Gospel and the reading from the Torah, Prophets, and Writings relate in one of three ways.[7]

1. Parallelism. Material from the Gospel is *parallel* in theological and/or ethical content with the passage from the Torah, Prophets, and Writings.

2. Contrast. Material from the Gospel *contrasts* with the theological and/or ethical content of the passage from the Torah, Prophets, and Writings.

3. Typology. The passage from the Torah, Prophets, and Writings is a *type*, foreshadowing, promise, or prophecy of the material in the Gospel.

From week to week in the two great cycles, the preacher must identify which one of these relationships prevails. When preaching from the paired readings in Ordinary Time, the preacher must make a similar determination.

The preacher should reflect theologically on this relationship: is it appropriate to the preacher's deepest convictions about God's purposes, especially with regard to the relationship of Judaism and Christianity?

Biblical Materials in the Lectionary

The following table gives a general indication of the distribution of Bible readings across the lectionary. Because each synoptic Gospel is prominent in one year, Year A is sometimes called the Year of Matthew, Year B is called the Year of Mark, and Year C the Year of Luke. Readings from the Fourth Gospel are scattered throughout the two major cycles and Ordinary Time.

	Year A	Year B	Year C
Synoptic Gospel	Matthew	Mark	Luke
Letters for semicontinuous reading in Ordinary Time (including Acts, Hebrews, Revelation)	After Epiphany Day: 1 Corinthians; after Easter: Acts; after Pentecost Day; Romans, Philippians, 1 Thessalonians	After Epiphany Day: 1 and 2 Corinthians; after Easter: 2 Corinthians, Acts after Pentecost Day: Ephesians, James, Hebrews	After Epiphany Day: 1 Corinthians; after Easter: Book of Revelation, Acts; after Pentecost Day:, Galatians, Colossians, 1 and 2 Timothy, 2 Thessalonians
Torah, Prophets, and Writing for semicontinuous reading in Ordinary Time after Pentecost Day	Ancestral narratives from Genesis, Moses the exodus, entering the Promised Land	Covenant with David, wisdom literature	Prophets (focusing on Jeremiah)
Gospel of John	John appears in Christmas, Lent, after Easter, and Pentecost Day	John appears in Advent, Christmas, Lent, the Sundays after Easter, Pentecost Day, Trinity Sunday, and continuous reading of John 6 in Ordinary Time	John appears in Lent, Christmas, after Epiphany, Lent, Easter, after Easter, Pentecost Day, Trinity Sunday

Strengths of the Revised Common Lectionary

Given the many strengths of the *Revised Common Lectionary*, it is not surprising that some preachers claim they will never start from any other point. Ironically, however, as we will see in the next chapter, nearly every strength has a corresponding weakness.

Exposes the Congregation to Many Parts of the Bible

One of the strongest aspects of the RCL is that it exposes the congregation to many parts of the Bible. Indeed, the lectionary contains readings from fifty-eight of the sixty-six books in the Protestant canon.[8] The breadth of coverage is especially far-reaching in the Gospels and Letters (twenty-four of the twenty-seven books appear). Moreover, over the three-year cycle, the congregation hears extensive parts of the synoptic Gospels and several of the letters.[9]

More important than how many books are included is the breadth of texts: the lectionary seeks to represent the stories of Israel, Jesus, and the church—creation, fall, ancestral narratives, exodus, Promised Land, judges, monarchy, divided monarchy, exile and return, life as a colony of Persia, Jesus, Paul and his followers, the later writers, and Revelation. The table of readings includes 107 of 150 psalms as well as excerpts from the writings.[10]

Such exposure is important in its own right since the Bible is central to the life of the church. A working knowledge of the content of the Bible, and methods of interpreting it, is crucial whether a congregation regards the Bible as its only theological authority or thinks of the Bible as a significant theological resource for dialogue with other sources of theological insight.

Exposure to the Bible in worship is further important because the sermon has become one of the most significant educational moments in long-established churches. In many congregations, Sunday school is declining, and even disappearing, especially among adults. Other efforts to help encourage members toward conversation with the Bible typically attract relatively few people. By itself, preaching from the *Revised Common Lectionary* cannot get the Bible into the soul of a congregation, but it does give the church a weekly opportunity to consider a broad swath of texts and themes.

Opens the Door to Considering the Diversity of the Biblical Writings

Preachers and scholars notice the diversity of biblical writings. The RCL opens the door for the preacher to help the congregation recognize and respond to the many different kinds of biblical writings.

Virtually all biblical scholars agree that the biblical materials came to expression in different times and places, and exhibit different literary characteristics. Think of the differences in style and function among the sagas of Genesis, the oracles of salvation and condemnation in the prophets, the hymnic qualities of the psalms, the wisdom sayings, the letters of Paul, and the apocalypse (book of Revelation). These genres contain multiple subcategories, each with its own qualities and purposes.

Many church leaders also believe that the Bible contains different theological points of view. I often speak of seven theological families in the Bible: Elohist, Yahwist, priestly, Deuteronomistic, wisdom, apocalyptic, and theology influenced by Hellenistic Judaism.[11] While these families share certain foundational perspectives, they also have their own distinct angles of perception. Moreover, there are differences among writers within each family.

The RCL encourages the preacher to consider not only the different styles of biblical literature, but also their different theological perspectives. The preacher can thus help the congregation compare and contrast the strengths and limitations of each theological voice, and can help the congregation consider which theological families are more and less helpful for the early twenty-first-century church.

When left to choose their own texts for preaching, ministers often exhibit preferences for a limited spectrum of biblical material. Indeed, some preachers have a "canon within the canon," that is, a small part of the Bible that actually functions more authoritatively for them than other parts. Preachers sometimes deliberately choose these foci, but preachers often develop such tendencies by default. Returning again and again to the same biblical material limits the congregation's awareness of the theological possibilities posed by the breadth and depth of biblical literature.

The larger work of the preacher is to help the congregation articulate what it most deeply believes about God and God's purposes and identify responses. From a postmodern angle, each text is an other, an entity with its own integrity. As the congregation moves toward identifying its core convictions, a preacher needs to help the congregation ponder the possibilities for understanding God offered in different theological families and different biblical passages.

Symbolizes the Preacher's Intention to be Faithful to Something Larger

Preachers sometimes (unconsciously) fall into perspectives that are too limited. We so concentrate on the immediate felt needs of the congregation that we lose sight of the bigger needs of the world and the deeper needs of the congregation to become more aware of God's presence and leading and to be more faithful in response. We sometimes preach our theologies in isolation from other theological visions. Even within our own theologies we sometimes return again and again to the same limited themes.

The *Revised Common Lectionary*, being outside the preacher, represents the importance of remembering that the preacher's theological focus and resources are not limited to the immediate situation and to the preacher's own theology. Preaching from the lectionary can symbolize the preacher's intention to be faithful to God in ways that are larger than meeting the congregation's immediate needs, and to draw from resources more numerous and nuanced than the preacher's private theology.

Simply following the lectionary does not guarantee that preachers can transcend their immediate perceptions or their own biases and blind spots. Indeed, preachers can use the lectionary to reinforce those very things. But an alert preacher may hear the lectionary tapping on the study window with a reminder to look outside at the larger world and resources of God.

Designed to Work with the Sacred Meal

The liturgical reform that began with the Second Vatican Council sought to recover both word and table as the double focus of worship. The trail of lectionary development that led to the *Revised Common Lectionary* intends for the Bible readings to have their fullest exposition in the presence of the Sacred Meal and for the presence of the risen Jesus in the Sacred Meal to be more manifest in preaching.

My own movement—the Christian Church (Disciples of Christ)— keeps the Feast every week. The preacher often ends the sermon by making a connection between the sermon and the loaf and the cup. When the sermon does not mention the Supper, the person who presides at the table often connects the sermon to the Meal when inviting people to the table.

In congregations that do not break the bread and pour the cup each week, the presence of the lectionary is a reminder of the presence of the living God as that presence would be manifest through the loaf and the cup. While the reading of the Bible and its interpretation through preaching is not, in my view, a substitute for eating the bread and drinking the cup, lectionary-based preaching can both evoke the sense of the Sacred Meal and can create a hunger for the real thing.

Encourages Preachers to Deal with Texts They Might Avoid

My tendency as a preacher is to turn away from difficult texts. Some texts are difficult because their historical, cultural, or literary settings are unfamiliar to people today. To ascertain what the texts meant in antiquity, the preacher must spend quite a bit of time in commentaries, Bible dictionaries, and other interpretive helps. Some texts seem to ask the followers of Jesus and the church to do things that are hard to do, such as love one's enemies. Beyond that, some texts are difficult because they asked people in antiquity to believe and do things that raise theological and ethical questions for the congregation today. Indeed, some passages in the Bible describe God acting in ways that I consider inappropriate and even repulsive.

However, by way of personal testimony, I have found that taking up a difficult text often becomes a peak preaching experience. Sometimes the reward is a wonderful sense of discovery when the text is hard to understand because of its unfamiliar historical associations. I delve into the commentaries and Bible dictionaries and, *voila*: a fresh sense of what the text meant in antiquity. Sometimes the reward comes from taking the risk of the text, such as inviting the congregation to consider loving their enemies. Sometimes the reward comes from struggling with a text that makes a troubling theological or ethical claim. Facing such a text forces me to think carefully about what I really believe (and do not believe).

By facing a difficult text openly and honestly, a preacher models the kind of theological reflection that enables a congregation to move from surface to deeper levels of conviction. Even when members of the congregation come to different conclusions, the shared struggle creates a sense of community.

Opportunity to Hear the Torah, Prophets, and Writings

The church is in a strange situation with respect to the Torah, Prophets, and Writings. On the one hand, the Torah and Prophets were considered sacred scripture in Judaism by the time of Jesus, and the Writings were on the way to the same status. Jesus and his earliest disciples were Jewish and were thus shaped by this literature and by the religious practices and culture of Judaism. Jesus and his disciples were faithfully Jewish. We can understand Jesus, the disciples, and the early church only through the lens of the Torah, Prophets, and Writings, and through Jewish culture and religious life.

On the other hand, some followers of Jesus began to devalue both Judaism and the Torah, Prophets, and Writings. This trend reached its nadir in Marcion (85 to 160 CE), who rejected the Torah, Prophets, and Writings because he believed they pictured a God of legalism and wrath whereas the God of Jesus was a deity of grace, compassion, and love. In his canon Marcion included only edited versions of the Gospel of Luke and some of Paul's letters. While Marcion's viewpoint was extreme, many Christians and churches from then through today have regarded the Torah, Prophets, and Writings as inferior. The diminution of the Torah, Prophets, and Writings contributes to anti-Judaism (prejudice against Jews), the more viral anti-Semitism (systematic hatred of Jews), and supersessionism (the idea that the church has superseded or replaced Judaism).

Many Christians today are unfamiliar with the actual content of the Torah, Prophets, and Writings. While few go as far as Marcion, many have a negative perception of those writings. Indeed, when I lead Bible studies in local congregations, I continue to hear people refer to the judgmental God of the Torah, Prophets, and Writings and to legalistic Judaism. Some Christians believe that religious fulfillment is possible only through Christian faith. Some congregations almost never hear the Torah, Prophets, and Writings in worship.

The *Revised Common Lectionary* brings the Torah, Prophets, and Writings before the congregation. Each week, the pastor has the opportunity to preach from such a text, and during Ordinary Time after Pentecost Day, the preacher can follow the Torah, Prophets, and Writings semi-continuously. The congregation thus has opportunities (1) to become acquainted with some of the content of the Torah, Prophets, and Writings; (2) to explore the relationship between the Gospels and Letters and the Torah, Prophets, and Writings; (3) to discover the true nature of Judaism as a religion of grace, justice, and love; and (4) to consider possibilities for shared mission between Judaism and the church.

Encourages Consciousness of the Theological Lens through Which the Preacher Interprets the Bible

A good many Christians think they simply read the Bible as the Bible. Such folk believe they read scripture in pure, objective, uninterpreted ways. However, as we observed in the preface to this book, all awareness takes place through the lenses of our social and theological locations. The categories of the Christian year are part of the social location of the preacher who follows the year. The preacher's theological family is also a key part of the preacher's social and theological location.

While preaching from the lectionary in the context of the Christian year does not mandate preachers to become conscious of interpreting the Bible

43

from their theological locations, the fact of the theological categories of the Christian year gives preachers an opportunity to become aware that they are not simply preaching from the Bible but are preaching from the Bible through the lenses of Advent, Christmas, Epiphany, Lent, Easter, Pentecost, and Ordinary Time.

Moreover, the lectionary preacher does not simply approach the Bible through the pure lens of the Christian year but interprets the Bible through a double theological lens: the Christian year and the preacher's more specific theological family. A preacher may interpret the lectionary texts from the theological frames of liberal theology, mutual critical correlation, process theology, fundamental or evangelical approaches, neo-orthodoxy, post-liberalism, liberation theology, theologies of otherness, racial/ethnic theologies, or combinations thereof. The more conscious we can be of our theological lenses, the more we can think critically about how those lenses shape our interpretation of God's presence and leading.

Combines Both Selected and Continuous Reading

The *Revised Common Lectionary* offers the values of both lectionary worlds—selected and continuous. Per chapter 1, a major strength of a selected lectionary is that its readings correlate with the themes of the Christian year. In the two seasons that tell the story of redemption—Advent–Christmas–Epiphany Day and Lent–Easter–Pentecost Day—the passages in the *Revised Common Lectionary* are selected because they help the church consider the theological themes of the seasons. The lections are thus chosen because they make specific contributions to Christian life as interpreted by the Christian year (and the lectionary committee).

Per the beginning of this chapter, a major strength of a continuous lectionary is that it brings the congregation into systematic contact with a significant body of biblical literature. The *Revised Common Lectionary* makes modified use of this principle by reading continuously or semi-continuously in the seasons of ordinary time both after Epiphany and Pentecost Days. Each year, a different synoptic Gospel is read semi-continuously in these parts of the year, as are letters or parts of letters. After Pentecost Day, one of the two sets of readings from a psalm and a Torah, Prophet, and Writing is semi-continuous: in Year A, ancestral narratives and the exodus; in Year B the covenant with David and wisdom literature; in Year C, the prophets.

In addition to the theological strengths just named, the two patterns of reading can add variety to both the preacher's preparation and the congregation's hearing. The change of pace of moving from one type of lectionary, table to another can help both preacher and community remain freshly alert to the possibilities of each approach.

Often Fits the Congregation and Its Context

The introductions to this book and this chapter cite a comment by a lectionary preacher which many ministers find true: "I can't believe how texts in the lectionary match up so well with the situation in our congregation right now." At times when I have been preaching from the lectionary, I have looked at the readings assigned for the upcoming Sunday and thought, "I could not have found better selections for our situation if I had thumbed through the Bible for a week."

At other times, the relationship between the texts and the context of the congregation is not immediately clear, but by living with texts in the context of the community, preachers begin to see connections below the surface. The preacher can then sometimes begin the sermon in an engaging and even fun way. For example: "When I first looked at the reading for today, I could not imagine what in the world it has to do with our setting right now..."

Such experiences testify to a remarkable quality of the Bible. Its stories, ideas, images, and themes often connect with life today in deep, complex ways. A biblical text can resonate with people in a variety of situations. When I was in Bible college, seminary, and graduate school in the late 1960s and early 1970s, scholars often spoke of *the* meaning of a biblical text. Soon, however, we began speaking of multivalence—the idea that a text does not have a single meaning but that people at different moments in life become sensitive to different aspects of biblical texts. Even after having taught the Bible for thirty years in a theological seminary, I look at texts I have taught many times and think, "I have never before seen that aspect of the text." Lectionary preachers often have their own versions of this experience.

Of course, the impending deadline of Sunday's sermon sometimes causes preachers to think they see things in a lectionary reading that are not really there. The multivalence of the Bible does not legitimate *every* interpretation. All interpretations need to be plausible from the standpoint of what might have been possible in antiquity.

A Place to Start Each Week

The *Revised Common Lectionary* gives the preacher a place to start sermon preparation. Preachers who must choose a preaching text each week sometimes flip and flop and flounder among texts before settling on one as the starting point for sermon preparation. "Should I turn to this text...or should I turn to that one...and what about this passage I vaguely remember, but not quite...?"

The lectionary gives the preacher a place to start. The preacher can move immediately to sermon preparation—exegesis, theological reflection, and considering hermeneutical and homiletical possibilities. To be sure, the preacher must choose a focus from the assigned texts for the day, but this range of choices is smaller than the pondering of the Bible as a whole.

Sunday School Curriculum Can Be Based on the Revised Common Lectionary

In a move that helps tie Sunday school and worship together and make them mutually reinforcing, a congregation can base its Sunday school curriculum and other educational enterprises on the *Revised Common Lectionary*. Students in the classroom on Sunday morning, or perhaps in educational or other programmatic events during the week, can study the passage(s) on which the sermon is based. *Seasons of the Spirit* is an example of such an approach. It is a lectionary-based resource for worship, faith formation, and service.[12] Week by week, *Seasons* provides planning guides, resources for biblical interpretation and for reflection, poetry and prose appropriate for the day, suggestions for stations for interacting with the text, activity sheets, and worship outlines.

Facilitates Long-Range Planning for Preaching

The RCL can facilitate long-range sermon planning. A preacher can identify biblical texts from which to preach for a month, three months, six months, or a year. Such planning helps the preacher begin to think not only about foci for sermons but also about how messages might work together over time for cumulative effect.[13]

While the immediate pressure of next Sunday's sermon often mobilizes the preacher's homiletical creativity, such pressure can also cause a preacher to bypass some possibilities or to grab desperately at others that are ill conceived. Being free from the immediate pressure of next Sunday's deadline may give the mind of the preacher time to work unconsciously on sermon topics. In the fall, we put the leaves from our trees in a compost pile. By spring, the leaves have turned to mulch, which we then use to enrich the soil elsewhere. Similarly, the preacher can put texts in a compost part of the mind. Returning to the sermon, the preacher may find homiletical mulch waiting.

An Abundance of Sermon Helps

The lectionary has generated an abundance of preaching helps. These resources include guides for exegesis, explorations of theology and herme- neutical issues, consideration of pastoral matters, catalogues of stories, as well as media presentations related to the lectionary (for example, paintings, poems, movies), and even sermons. Such resources come in a variety of formats—books, journals, DVDs, websites, blogs, and more. The preacher can subscribe to such material or get it free in libraries and on websites and can contribute, especially through the Internet. Ministers have never had access to so many sermon helps in the entire history of preaching. Sitting at my computer, I can open a dozen resources for next Sunday in seconds. Click. Click. Click.

Facilitates Sermon Preparation Groups among Clergy Colleagues and Members of the Congregation

Many clergy who follow the RCL meet together in small groups for sermon preparation.[14] The members bring their own perspectives and thus enlarge an individual preacher's perception of possibilities. Members often benefit from talking with other preachers about questions, issues, insights, and potential directions.

The lectionary gives the group an immediate focus. The format, fre- quency, and place to meet vary from group to group. In some groups, one member starts the discussion with ideas about exegesis, theology, hermeneu- tics, and directions for the sermon for one lesson, or for all lessons. In other groups, each member takes a particular task each week. Occasional groups have no structure. Meetings nearly always include time for all participants to raise questions, share insights, and mention possible resources (such as documentaries or movies). Some groups meet weekly, others monthly, still others quarterly. Groups sometimes take lectionary planning retreats. A group may meet in a church building, a library, a coffee shop, or a park. The clergy life can often be lonely. Such groups not only provide immediate help in sermon preparation but also become communities of support.

The lectionary can thus be an important resource for preaching. How- ever, as we will see in the next chapter, the lectionary is not the only starting point for sermon preparation.

47

CHAPTER 3

Preaching from the *Revised Common Lectionary*: Cautions

As noted earlier, in discussions with ministers who follow the *Revised Common Lectionary*, I often hear appreciation for the lectionary tinged with restlessness about it. Some pastors are specific about their questions, while others have a feeling that, for all its good, the lectionary has some rough edges.

I hope this chapter helps ministers name concerns about the *Revised Common Lectionary*. This chapter seeks to expand the critical reflection on the RCL that began in the preceding chapter by raising some cautions about the lectionary. Some of these issues are connected as much with how the church uses the lectionary as they are with the lectionary itself, but some are inherent in the lectionary.[1]

Never Hearing the Sweep of the Continuous Biblical Story

The previous chapter praises the lectionary for exposing the congregation to a lot of the Bible. However, this aspect of the lectionary has a shadow side. The lectionary *never* presents the sweep of the biblical story in one continuous narrative. Indeed, as we have frequently pointed out, the major *categories of the Christian year* become the lens through which the congregation encounters the Bible.

While the congregation reads parts of the Bible semi-continuously in Ordinary Time—the Gospels and Letters, and possibly parts of the Torah, Prophets, and Writings—the congregation never hears the biblical narrative in sequence from Genesis through Revelation. Indeed, when the Christian year reaches its theological climaxes in the Advent–Christmas–Epiphany Day and Lent–Easter–Pentecost Day seasons, the selected lections are presented without any sense of overarching narrative context. From week to week we can bounce from one text (and one world) to another.

The Bible in its canonical form is presented as a single story from creation through Israel to Jesus, the church, and the coming of a new world. While the diversity of biblical materials reminds us that the story can be interpreted in different ways, there are some deep common themes portraying the character and purposes of God and how human communities can live in partnership with God and one another. Indeed, the story of Jesus makes fullest sense only within the larger story of God's purposes in Israel, which itself only makes its fullest sense within the yet larger story of God's purposes in creation.

To be sure, individual biblical writers tell their parts of the story with particular nuances—sometimes even in conflict with one another—but the canon keeps them together as part of one *über*-story. For instance, although the books of the Deuteronomistic Samuels and Kings deal with many of the same characters and events as the priestly Chronicles, the two sets of books nuance characters, events, and theological perspectives quite differently.

Furthermore, awareness of the overarching story of the Bible gives the congregation a framework within which to place the individual readings in the lectionary. To understand the admonitions of Ezra-Nehemiah for the people of Israel to refrain from marrying gentiles, we need to know that Jewish community was in danger of being assimilated into Persian culture after the return from exile.

Overarching knowledge of the biblical narrative is especially helpful when Israel or the church has given the present form to a text at a time that is out of sequence from the place of the story as told in the canon. For example, although Sarah and Abraham probably lived about 1800 BCE, the priestly theologians gave their story its present form at the time of the exile (597–533 BCE). The priestly writers shaped the story of Sarah and Abraham to speak to their later day. These theologians wanted the Jewish people to identify with the ancestral couple and to hear the story as God's promise to the exiles. As God made good on the promises to Sarah and Abraham, so God would make good on the promises to the exiles. From this point of view, the congregation ideally should know not only the great arc of the biblical narrative but also when particular biblical texts were given their present form in relationship to that arc.

Preaching, of course, cannot bear the sole responsibility for helping a congregation become familiar with the breadth and depth of the biblical stories. But preaching needs to do its part, especially in view of the fact that worship is the primary place where many Christians in long-established churches encounter the Bible today.

Chapter 4 will pose ways for the congregation to read through representative texts in their internal biblical narrative and in the chronology in which they were actually given their present form. Such approaches encourage regular attenders to develop a feel for the biblical narrative as a whole.

Diminishes the Otherness of the Bible

Respect for the other is one of the most potent themes in contemporary philosophy, theology, and ethics.[2] The other is any entity—individual human being, particular community, element of nature, even a text—that is different from me. When we recognize the genuine otherness of the other—how different the other is from oneself—the encounter with the other has the power to open us to fresh and often transforming perspectives on ourselves, our communities, our relationships with the others, and the world. The other presents us with possibilities we may not have imagined. At its best, recognizing the other enriches our awareness of the diversity of the human and natural worlds. Taking seriously the otherness of the other works against the tendency of many human beings to interpret others as extensions of ourselves, as reflections of our own values and behaviors.

In optimum situations, the Bible (with its multifaceted theological and cultural diversity) functions as an other by bringing us into the presence of ideas about God, the world, and the faithful life that cause us to recognize possibilities we may not have previously considered. Indeed, encounters with the Bible can be transforming with respect to alerting people to the nature of God, the divine purposes in the world, and the possibilities that result when we respond appropriately and inappropriately.

The preacher needs to tread thoughtfully here. On the one hand, students and preachers sometimes speak about the Bible in such glowing terms a congregation could be forgiven for thinking the Bible has theological radium at its core. Seeking to respect the otherness of the Bible does not mean that every text in the Bible is a model for theology and ethical prescription. The Bible contains theological and ethical perspectives that trouble many people, at least on surface reading. We need to avoid romanticizing the Bible even as we need to avoid simply bypassing biblical materials that are problematic. Coming face-to-face with the otherness of biblical texts that raise theological and ethical questions can help the church think deeply and helpfully about what the church truly believes and does.

However, in the context of the Christian year and the *Revised Common*

Lectionary, the otherness of the Bible is filtered through the theology of the Christian year. The church does not read the Bible as the Bible but reads the Bible as the Bible serves the themes of the Christian year. The preacher approaches the Bible through theological categories secondary to the biblical readings themselves. This phenomenon is particularly true during the two pivotal cycles of Advent–Christmas–Epiphany Day and Lent–Easter–Pentecost Day.[3] In Advent, for instance, the preacher is supposed to ask how the Bible passages help us understand and prepare for the coming of Christ (both the second coming and in remembrance of the first coming).[4]

As confirmed elsewhere, we can never encounter the otherness of the Bible in pure and unfiltered ways. However, we can try to look at biblical texts being as mindful of our interpretive inclinations as possible. To honor the particular otherness of a biblical passage, a pastor preaching from the lectionary may want to set aside the theological constraints of the Christian year and focus on the text as text.

Disadvantages the Torah, Prophets, and Writings

While one strength of the *Revised Common Lectionary* is to bring passages from the Torah, Prophets, and Writings into the purview of the congregation, this gain is counterbalanced by the losses incurred by the way the Torah, Prophets, and Writings appear in the lectionary. These disadvantages feed prejudice against the Torah, Prophets, and Writings; supersessionism in Christian theology; and anti-Jewish and anti-Semitic inclinations latent in many congregations.

The Torah, Prophets, and Writings have a much smaller place in the *Revised Common Lectionary* than they do in the Bible. While the Torah, Prophets, and Writings make up about 75 percent of the Protestant Bible, readings from the Torah, Prophets, and Writings (counting the Psalms) make up only about 50 percent of the lectionary. If the Psalms, intended for liturgical use, are factored out, readings from the Torah, Prophets, and Writings make up only about 33 percent of the lections.

An even greater disadvantage is the fact that in congregations that read the three main lessons each week, the people hear two readings from the Gospels and Letters and only one passage from the Torah, Prophets, and Writings. I estimate that about 70 percent of the content of the Gospels and Letters but only about 20 percent of the content of the Torah, Prophets, and Writings appears in the lectionary.

We have already noted that the congregation never hears the overarching narrative of creation, the primeval history, and the story of Israel in a continuous series of readings. Furthermore, except when the preacher focuses on semi-continuous readings from the Torah, Prophets, and Writings in Ordinary Time, the readings from the Torah, Prophets, and Writings are always secondary to the Gospel. Thus, when the theology of the Christian year is clearest and when attendance at worship is the highest in Advent–Christmas–Epiphany Day and Lent–Easter–Pentecost Day, the church practically never hears the Torah, Prophets, and Writings in their own voices. Instead, the congregation views the latter materials primarily in relationship to the Gospel and the Letters.

The Sundays after Easter betray the lectionary's underlying attitude toward the Torah, Prophets, and Writings. The resurrection of Jesus, of course, is the single most important event in the ministry of Jesus, as it both confirms God's approval of Jesus and also embodies the character of the life that God intends for all. Yet, on the Sundays after Easter, when the Christian Year calls upon the church to reflect over seven Sundays on the significance of the resurrection, the lectionary continues the psalm but *drops* the reading from the Torah, Prophets, and Writings and replaces it with a passage from Acts. While it is good to read from Acts, with its stirring picture of the life of the community of the resurrection, preachers and worship planners should add a reading from the Torah, Prophets, and Writings to represent continuity between the work of God pictured in those writings and the work of God through the resurrection.

As noted in the previous chapter, when the RCL pairs a reading from the Torah, Prophets, and Writings with a reading from the Gospel, the lectionary assumes one of three relationships between the two passages: parallel, contrast, and typology. The *parallel* relationship is the most theologically satisfactory since the readings present God acting in both Israel and the ministry of Jesus in a parallel fashion. The relationship of *contrast* is the most theologically problematic since the contrast is often between inferior Judaism and superior Christianity. The relationship of *typology* leans toward being theologically unsatisfactory since it often presumes that the material in the reading from the Torah, Prophets, and Writings is a type or prophecy that is fulfilled only in the ministry of Jesus and the life of the church. Contrast and typology functionally assume that God's work in Judaism is incomplete and that the Jewish community is a second-rate religious body. In my view, the preacher often needs to offer theological criticism of the relationships of contrast and typology and to expose the anti-Judaism that lies in the background of such categories.[5]

The psalms are more represented in the *Revised Common Lectionary* than

53

any other part of the Torah, Prophets, and Writings, with excerpts from 107 of 150 psalms in the table of readings. While the psalms are intended more for liturgical use than for preaching, preachers sometimes find the psalm to be an ideal trailhead for a sermon. In many congregations, the psalm is read or sung every week, even when it is unrelated to the sermon. Several of the psalms are repeated in whole or in part in the lectionary two, three, four, five, and even six times.

However, while many psalms are exalted in their declamations about God, a significant number of psalms put forward theologically and ethically problematic statements. While the lectionary committee has not assigned many of the most difficult passages, some difficult passages are left in place. Moreover, the *Revised Common Lectionary* omits (or assigns as alternate readings) some psalms that are important for understanding Jesus and the Gospels and Letters. For example, Psalm 2, which is crucial to interpreting the baptism of Jesus as well as the title "son of God," appears in the table of readings only as an alternate reading. Psalm 110, which is pivotal for understanding the notion of the resurrected Jesus at the right hand of God, does not appear at all.

Sometimes Violates the Natural Beginning and Ending Points of the Readings

One of the most basic principles of biblical interpretation is to identify the natural beginning and ending points of a text so as to honor the theological and literary integrity of the text. Scholars urge preachers to identify a meaningful unit of the Bible as the center of the sermon. While most of the readings in the lectionary are holistic units for interpretation, some texts start and stop in ways that violate the integrity of the text.

Such violations appear to occur for three reasons. (1) Some complete literary sections are too long for public reading in worship. The lectionary committee sought to shorten the reading. For example, the story of the great flood encompasses Genesis 6:1–9:17. An interpretation of any part of the text requires knowledge of the entire story. Yet, three and a half chapters is too long to read aloud in worship. For Proper 4, Year A, the lectionary assigns Genesis 6:9-22; 7:24; and 8:14-19. (2) The lectionary wishes to heighten the attention given to occasional texts. Luke 4:14-30, Jesus' inaugural sermon in the synagogue at Nazareth, for instance, is a complete unit of Lucan theology. The lectionary, however, breaks the text into two parts: Luke 4:14-20 (Jesus reading from the prophet Isaiah, "The Spirit of the Lord is upon me…") and Luke 4:21-30 (God sent prophets to the widow of Zarephath and Naaman the Syrian). (3) The lectionary edits out some material that is theologically or ethically problematic. Psalm 9:9-20, for example, appears with the semi-continuous reading on Proper 7 in Year B. I suspect the reading begins with verse 9 because verses 1-8 portray the psalmist exulting because God has caused the psalmist's enemies to perish, blotting out their names forever and ever. These behaviors—God killing and the psalmist rejoicing over the killing—are hardly the stuff of compassion and love. As we point out in the following section, such texts provide the preacher with gripping points of entry into theological reflection.

A part of the preacher's calling is to determine where to begin and end the biblical text. Most of the time, when the lectionary assigns boundaries that are arbitrary or misleading, a preacher can change the starting and ending points so the preacher is working with a meaningful unit. To fail to do so is to allow the lectionary to be the master of the church and not the servant of the larger purposes of God.

When a passage is too long to be read in worship, the preacher can read important parts and summarize other parts so the congregation gets a sense of the text as a whole. The preacher wants to be sure to read those elements of the text that are fundamental to the sermon.

Steers the Preacher Away from Many of the Most Difficult Texts

The previous chapter cites steering the preacher toward texts that the preacher might otherwise avoid as a strength of the lectionary. The other side of the coin is that the *Revised Common Lectionary* steers the preacher away from many of the most difficult texts. The lectionary simply does not assign some passages that raise the most enervating theological and ethical issues. A classic text in this regard is Psalm 137. The lectionary appoints verses 1-7 of this soulful lamentation from the time when the Babylonians had destroyed Jerusalem and sent its leaders into exile: "By the rivers of Babylon—there we sat down, and there we wept when we remembered Zion" (v. 1). Many people who have suffered loss identify with the lament in verses 1-7. However, the lection does not include verses 8-9: "O daughter Babylon, you devastator! Happy shall they be who pay you back what you have done to us! Happy shall they be who take your little ones and dash them against the rock!"

Many preachers are relieved when the lectionary excises such passages. "I don't have to struggle with that text this week. Whew." However, such relief is often misplaced. Readings like Psalm 137:8-9 force the preacher and congregation to ask some of the most foundational theological questions: "What do we most deeply believe about God, God's purposes, and appropriate responses?" The congregation needs to consider the degree to which they believe God wills both the deaths of innocent children, and rejoicing on the part of those who put them to death. Indeed, while we may understand the depth of bitterness that gave rise to Psalm 137:8-9, its sentiment is theologically repugnant. Preaching on such texts forces preacher and congregation to think carefully about why they find it so.

To take other examples, the lectionary omits Romans 1:18-32, with its stark portrayal of same-gender relationships. In our time when the church is tied up in knots over that issue, such an omission is criminal. The lectionary does not include 1 Corinthians 14:33b-36, with its infamous injunction for women to be silent in the churches. Indeed, the lectionary gives little attention to similar injunctions elsewhere in the Letters. At a time when the church is still unsettled about women in leadership, leaving out such passages is dismaying.

Preachers and worship planners can reclaim passages that raise searching theological and ethical questions by expanding the boundaries of some existing lections and by adding some passages to the lectionary readings. Indeed, as noted in connection with the Christian year, struggling with such biblical material can ultimately become some of the most meaningful sermons for both preacher and congregation.

Turning Sermons into Lectures on the Bible

Preachers who follow the lectionary sometimes turn sermons into lectures that provide information on understanding biblical texts in their ancient historical and literary contexts but that do not connect very much with today. The preacher seems to assume that a sermon has accomplished its purpose by clarifying what a text asked people to believe and do in the ancient world. I notice this phenomenon most often when the preacher tries to bring two, three, or even all four readings for the day into the sermon, and spends much of the sermon explaining the different texts and how they relate with one another. Of course, this phenomenon is not limited to preaching from the lectionary. It is found in other forms of preaching. This difficulty lies not in the lectionary itself but in the preacher's approach to the sermon.

One of my teachers, Edmund A. Steimle, of Union Theological Seminary in New York, had a proverb that speaks to this situation: "Preaching that starts in the Bible and stays in the Bible is not biblical." Preaching should not just explain the text from the past but should help the congregation interpret God's purposes in the present. While preachers are called to honor the otherness of the biblical text, the preacher's distinctive vocation is to help the congregation ponder how conversation with the text helps the congregation interpret and respond to God's presence and purposes today.

Reading Passages in Worship without Comment Can Be Perplexing, Even Dangerous

Some congregations read all three regular passages and the psalm every Sunday. A single sermon can seldom comment in sufficient exegetical depth on the three regular passages, much less adding the psalm into the mix. Some passages are simply read aloud without comment.

In some cases, hearing a text without interpretation is likely to be perplexing to the congregation. Hebrews 5:5-10, appointed for both the Fifth Sunday in Lent, Year B, and Proper 24, Year B, claims that Jesus is a priest "according to the order of Melchizedek." Given how little this figure occurs in the Bible, a congregation can be forgiven for wondering, "Who is Melchizidek, and what does it mean to be priest in his order, and why should we care?"

In other cases, the result of reading a passage without interpretation is potentially more troubling. Many Christians assume—some naively but others as a result of consciously chosen commitments—that the Bible is an entirely reliable source of theological guidance. They think they should believe what a passage says, and do what it prescribes. First Peter 2:19-25 appears on the Fourth Sunday of Easter in Year A and says, "It is a credit to you if, being aware of God, you endure pain while suffering unjustly." Hearing this passage by itself, a congregation could take this text as urging people who suffer injustice simply to accept their situation and not to protest.

Given such possibilities, my recommendation is that a congregation read aloud (or print in the bulletin) only the text(s) on which the preacher can comment adequately in the message. Congregations have incredible staying power as institutions. Chances are that texts not read aloud this year can come to voice in public worship in three years, when the lectionary year comes around again. At that time, the preacher might address the text with the necessary exegetical, theological, and hermeneutical attention. If a congregation is committed to reading every text every Sunday, then the congregation could plan a teaching moment to set the historical context for each lesson and to offer brief but needful theological commentary on the lessons.

57

Sometimes Overlooks Naturally Resonant Pairs of Readings from the Torah, Prophets, and Writings with Readings from the Gospels and Letters

Many texts in the Gospels and Letters presume direct relationship with passages from the Torah, Prophets, and Writings. Lections from the Gospels and Letters sometimes directly quote, paraphrase, or echo passages from the Torah, Prophets, and Writings. It makes exegetical sense to have such texts read together so the congregation can move toward appreciating the direct ways in which writers of the Gospels and Letters drew from the well of sacred Jewish literature. While the lectionary sometimes assigns such naturally resonant pairs on the same day, it often overlooks these connections. Indeed, the lectionary sometimes pairs texts whose relationship is arbitrary and even artificial.

When the *Revised Common Lectionary* bypasses an organic pairing, the preacher could simply replace the lectionary assignment for the Torah, Prophets, and Writings with a text from that body of literature that the Gospel or Letter quotes, paraphrases, or echoes. For instance, on the Second Sunday of Advent in Year A, the lectionary pairs Matthew 3:1-12 (John the Baptist preaching in the wilderness) with Isaiah 11:1-11 ("A shoot shall come out from the stump of Jesse" [v. 1 NRSV]). The Matthean passage, however, directly quotes Isaiah 40:3. It makes better exegetical sense, then, for the congregation to hear Isaiah 40:1-5 in connection with Matthew 3:1-12.

Such an effort is particularly important on the Sundays after Easter when the lectionary abandons the Torah, Prophets, and Writings and draws the third reading from the book of Acts. On the Fourth Sunday of Easter, Year B, John 10:11-18, "I am the good shepherd,' is paired with Acts 4:5-12, Peter and John before the council. The language of John 10:11-18 makes clear that John wants the congregation to whom the Fourth Gospel was written to hear that passage against the background of Ezekiel 34:1-31, with its contrast between the true and false shepherds of Israel. John wants the congregation to think of Jesus as the true shepherd and the leaders of the Pharisees as false shepherds. Reading Ezekiel in worship would open the door for the preacher to call attention to John's intent and to help the community reflect on the theological appropriateness of John's presentation.

Trying to Deal with Multiple Texts Can Confuse the Sermon

On some Sundays, the lections come from quite different periods of history, different geographical locations, different circumstances, different purposes for writing, and different theological perspectives. The exegetical, theological, and hermeneutical issues of each text deserve their own sermons. Yet, week by week some preachers try to bring all three paired texts (and even the psalm) into a single sermon. Trying to deal with too many texts can confuse a single sermon, especially when preachers try to find connections among texts where none exist.

One text usually raises enough issues for one sermon. Yet this rule is not absolute. A deft preacher might use two or three texts with different theological perspectives to help the congregation identify and evaluate the differences. A well-organized preacher might show how a theological trajectory evolves over two or even three texts or bodies of literature. But such efforts can be encouraged only when the preacher can move directly and clearly to the heart of the historical, literary, theological, and hermeneutical issues associated with each passage and with the interaction of the passages.

Can Be Hard to Tell the Readings Are Related to the Sacred Meal

While the *Revised Common Lectionary* in the context of the Christian year is intended to be part of a service of worship that includes both preaching and the Sacred Meal, this connection may not be self-evident to the typical congregation. Only a handful of the Bible readings actually refer to the loaf and the cup or to other occasions of eating and drinking. The table of readings does not directly refer to communion. While the lectionary may evoke the presence of the loaf and cup for the preacher, most members of the congregation will be aware only of the Bible readings as readings.

In a congregation that follows the RCL but does not eat at the Table every week, the preacher and worship leaders likely need to alert the congregation to this connection. Such information can be passed along in services of worship, in the worship bulletin, on the big screen, on the website, and elsewhere.

May Not Fit the Context

Preachers are often pleased by how well *Revised Common Lectionary* texts fit the moment in life for which a sermon is prepared. At times, however, the assigned texts are not optimum starting points in helping the preacher and congregation think theologically about something in the larger culture or in the congregation. At times, preachers could make their way from the lections to the context, but the amount of exegetical, theological, or hermeneutical effort required for a responsible message would eat up so much of the sermon, the preacher would not have enough time to help the congregation move toward meaningful interpretation of the situation. Such rough spots may occur in connection with isolated Sundays or across several weeks or even seasons of a congregation's life.

When the RCL gets in the way of the fundamental work of preaching—helping the congregation make theological sense of life—a preacher should feel the freedom to go outside the lectionary for biblical texts or for theological or topical foci from which to approach the situation. At the same time, departing from the lectionary raises its own cautions. A preacher must choose a text or other focus carefully so as to honor the integrity of the text. Moreover, the act of choosing a text or other focus can eat up a lot of time the preacher needs for more direct preparation of the sermon.

Tempted to Substitute Lectionary Helps for the Preacher's Own Study and Reflection

Preachers who rely too much on lectionary preaching helps can drift into laziness and irresponsibility. When turning to lectionary preaching helps, a preacher needs to exercise both discipline and caution. With respect to discipline, the preacher can too easily use such resources as a substitute for the preacher's own sermon preparation. When I was once a guest preacher, I approached the pulpit before the service to get a feel for that space and found the local preacher's manuscript from the previous Sunday: a printout of a sermon from a well-known website. To the preacher's credit, the preacher had changed a first-person story of a personal experience in the original printout to a third-person story, but otherwise, had evidently preached the sermon with little change.

The quality of lectionary helps varies. Some lectionary preaching aids are excellent in providing reliable and insightful comments into exegetical, theological, and hermeneutical matters, and on raising provocative questions for sermons. Many helps, however, are unreliable, and can even lead the preacher astray because of their shoddy or biased exegesis, theology, or hermeneutical perspective. Preachers should use particular caution when turning to lectionary helps from the Internet. While some excellent resources appear on the World Wide Web, some sites offer little more than the writer's prejudices given an elevated impression by clever web design.

Preachers are dishonest when they pass off another preacher's sermon as if it is their own. Even if a minister does not preach another person's sermon in its entirety, the preacher may lean too much on prepackaged lectionary helps, and thereby deny the congregation the local theological reflection it needs. As a matter of the ethics of preaching, ministers ought to prepare their own sermons. Of course, a preacher's encounter with responsible lectionary helps can be a generative encounter with others. In order to keep fresh, preachers might periodically want to monitor how they use lectionary preaching aids.

Has the Lectionary Really Helped?

I raise this matter less as a criticism and more as something to ponder. On the basis of naïve observation, I cannot tell that the use of the Christian year and the *Revised Common Lectionary* have substantially improved the theological consciousness or ethical witness of many congregations in the long-established churches that have come to follow the Christian year and the lectionary in my lifetime. Indeed, based on the level of theological and ethical discourse I hear in many congregations and in middle- and upper-level judicatories, I would say that the theological illiteracy evident in an earlier generation has not been greatly ameliorated by a generation or more of exposure to the Christian year and the lectionary.[6]

Moreover, from the standpoint of institutional vitality, one must note that the historic Protestant communities that use the Christian year and the lectionary have largely been in a state of decline since the 1970s. I do not imply that the Christian year and the lectionary have caused such decline. Perhaps the decline would have been more precipitous if such churches had not adopted the Christian year and the lectionary. But the Christian year and the lectionary do not seem to me to be sparking theological, ethical, or missional renaissance.

Faithfulness, not statistical proliferation, is the standard by which to measure the success of the church. Nevertheless, for the church to make a witness, it must have some warm bodies and thinking minds. The church needs to think critically about approaches to preaching and worship that embody theological integrity while being part of an approach to Christian life that is inviting to more people in the early twenty-first century. Otherwise, progressive Christian witness could eventually become little more than sect groups meeting here and there. To be sure, *God* is ever and always in the world and working for the world's good, and, according to Acts, God is never without witness in any time or place (14:17). But vibrant congregations help name and interpret the divine purposes for love, peace, justice, and abundance.[7]

In any event, the lectionary is a created entity. By definition, then, the lectionary is finite and partial. Only God is infinite and complete. To approach the lectionary as if it is infinite and complete is to make the lectionary an idol. The lectionary preacher's question is about the degree to which the lectionary can encourage the congregation toward life-giving interpretations of God's presence and leading.

Preaching through a Book of the Bible (Continuous Lectionary)

Many people read novels at night before going to sleep. Readers enter the world created in the novel beginning with the first sentence and go page by page through the book. The reader imagines the setting, identifies with the characters, experiences the plot, and ponders connections with (and distance from) the reader's own context. A careful reader does not flip through the book, looking at a paragraph here and there. Indeed, dipping randomly into a novel can create a mistaken impression of the work. While readers are sometimes caught by particular scenes, these scenes have their fullest impact in the narrative context of the novel. Moreover, the experience of reading a good novel is a part of the meaning of the novel; it adds to our experience in ways we cannot always name. In a similar way, most books of the Bible achieve their greatest impact when we read them from start to finish.

This chapter focuses on continuous reading and preaching as an approach that seeks to honor the historical, literary, and theological contexts of biblical books and the particular texts within. We begin by noting that continuous reading and preaching has a proven track record, by identifying several positive values in continuous preaching, and by naming some practical things to keep in mind when preaching in this mode. We also discuss semi-continuous preaching.[1]

While this chapter primarily uses the language of continuous reading and preaching, most of the values and practices associated with continuous preaching also apply to semi-continuous reading and preaching. A preacher might also take a continuous approach to parts of biblical books. However, as noted in the following pages, semi-continuous preaching and preaching continuously through parts of biblical books have their own small cautions.

The *Revised Common Lectionary* recognizes the values of continuous and semi-continuous approaches by appointing sequential readings of parts of many biblical books, and some entire books, in Ordinary Time.[2] The values and dangers of *lectio continua* thus apply to lectionary readings in those categories.

A Proven Track Record

Continuous reading and preaching of scripture has a proven track record in helping sustain identity and mission in Judaism and Christianity both in difficult moments and in everyday circumstances.[3] *Continua* is not the only approach to preaching with such a record, but few other approaches have proven generative in so many different times, places, and circumstances.

Roots in Judaism

While we cannot be sure when continuous reading and preaching appeared in Judaism, Nehemiah (about 445–433 BCE) seems to presuppose it when describing Ezra and his assistants reading sequentially through the Torah and giving "the sense, so that the people understood the reading" (Neh. 8:8). Continuous exposition flowered before the time of Jesus at Qumran in commentaries on Isaiah, Habakkuk, and other writings. The Targums, translations of the Torah, Prophets, and Writings from Hebrew into Aramaic, include interpretive perspectives woven continuously into the translation.[4] By the time of the Talmud, continuous reading was assumed (for example, Megillah 29a-32a; Baba Qamma 82a).[5] One of the many forms of rabbinic midrash (meaning, roughly, "interpretation") is commenting on texts from start to finish.[6] In synagogue worship to this day, the community reads through the Torah every year, accompanied by a selected reading from the Prophets. Continuous reading and preaching has thus helped sustain Judaism in the face of prejudice, harassment, forced relocation, pogroms, and genocide.

In the Church

We do not know when continuous reading and preaching began in the Christian community. However, as in Judaism, it shows a remarkable capacity to empower the church.[7] Origen (185–254 CE) is the first preacher about whom we have certain evidence of *continua* through his allegorical expositions of Genesis, Song of Songs, Matthew, John, Romans, and other writings. Augustine (354–430), Chrysostom (347–407), Gregory of Nyssa (330–395), and Gregory the Great (540–604) also followed this pattern.

Consistent with the principle of *sola scriptura* (scripture is the only norm by which to measure the church's beliefs and actions), continuous reading was an important part of the Reformation. Luther (1483–1546), Zwingli (1484–1531), Bucer (1491–1551), Calvin (1509–1564), John Knox (1514–1572), the Puritans, and others used the continuous pattern. Following books of the Bible from beginning to end helped sustain the Protestant church during the long and tumultuous time of finding its own identity.

Between the Reformation and the contemporary period, some churches followed *lectio continua* (especially in the Reformed tradition) while others practiced *lectio selecta* (notably Roman Catholics, Lutherans, and Anglicans). In the late eighteenth and nineteenth centuries, under the influence of revivalism and other factors, a good many preachers in North America shifted away from continuous reading and preaching. In the twentieth century, preaching based on one isolated passage of scripture chosen in connection with a topic became commonplace. Historians and theologians often critique this latter preaching as losing some of its biblical and theological depth and becoming captive to the values and practices of the culture.

Beginning in the mid-twentieth century, quite a few churches on the evangelical end of the theological spectrum began to recover continuous reading and preaching. Indeed, some such preaching circles speak about a revival of *lectio continua*. Many congregations in this theological stream exhibit a lot of theological vitality and missional energy. To be sure, continuous reading and preaching is not singularly responsible for congregational vitality. But *continua* seems to touch deep chords in the spiritual souls of numerous individuals and congregations.

Continuous reading and preaching is not captive to any one theological family. A minister can preach continuously through any theological lens. *Continua* may or may not be appropriate for a particular congregation's context, but we should not dismiss it uncritically.

Values of Preaching Continuously through Books of the Bible

There are several important reasons for preaching continuously through books of the Bible. These values are not all unique to such preaching, but their cumulative effect encourages the preacher to consider this approach.

65

Helps the Congregation Enter the World of the Biblical Book

The beginning of this chapter compares reading a good novel to reading a book of the Bible. In the same way a reader enters into the fullness of the world of the novel only by reading the entire novel, so a preacher and congregation enter the fullness of the world of a book of the Bible by reading (and preaching from) the entire book.

- By starting at the beginning and preaching through to the end, minister and listeners follow the plot or overarching structure and movement of the book, and thus have a framework within which to place individual texts. The congregation can see how the piece (the individual text) is given meaning by its place in the whole book, and how the whole receives meaning from the piece.

- The congregation can develop a sense of the big picture of the book as well as the major points it made in its historical and theological settings. The preacher is less likely to make too much or too little out of one passage.

- When characters, settings, actions, themes, images, actions, or ideas occur throughout the biblical material, pastor and people have an opportunity to encounter those elements in depth, and, when appropriate, to follow their development over the course of the book.

- All the biblical writers have their own nuances of style, expression, and theology. Moving sequentially through a book of the Bible gives the congregation the opportunity to pick up those nuances.

- From week to week, preachers can help the congregation fill their reservoir with ever-deepening knowledge about the world of the biblical book so their encounter with the text becomes correspondingly deeper.

- Continuous sermons give the preacher natural opportunities to explain points at which the biblical writers or editors gave material its particular shape over time in response to changing circumstances.

Continua works most easily with biblical books whose passages naturally flow one to another, such as narrative books, most of the prophetic books, and the Letters. Even with volumes whose principles of arrangement are less obvious (at least to the Western mind), following a book from beginning to end can be an important experience of otherness, and, hence, discovery.

Continuity in the Sermon from Week to Week

When sermons move from start to finish through a biblical book, the congregation has a sense of continuity in the sermon from week to week in much the same way that a reader has a sense of continuity when moving from one chapter in a novel to another. When preachers choose their own texts, or when they follow a selected lectionary, the congregation may jump from Sunday to Sunday not only from book to book but also from era to era, place to place, and circumstance to circumstance: from Ur in the Chaldees to Israel in slavery in Egypt to Jerusalem at the peak of its power during the monarchy to members of an occupied nation rebelling against Antiochus Epiphanes IV to an apocalyptic sect in the wake of the destruction to Jerusalem to Paul in prison in Rome. Good preachers help the congregation discern the context of the text each week. And a preacher's theological consistency should provide continuity from week to week. Nevertheless, the jump from one biblical setting to another can be jarring. Preaching through a biblical book keeps the congregation in the same historical, literary, and theological world from week to week and encourages listeners to keep building on what they have heard.

Models Good Interpretive Methods for the Congregation

Every approach to preaching models biblical and theological interpretive methods for the congregation. Some approaches model better methods than others, and I think preaching continuously increases the likelihood of helping members of the congregation develop trustworthy models of interpretation. An old exegetical proverb says: a text without context is pretext. Ministers often cite this principle when parishioners quote individual verses out of their larger biblical contexts, sometimes violating the plausible meanings of the verses. A version of the same thing can happen with respect to passages: a preacher or a congregation can violate a passage by pulling the passage as a whole out of its larger contexts.

Every form of biblical interpretation can be abused. But preaching continuously seems to me to increase the likelihood that a preacher will pay serious attention to the historical, literary, and theological contexts of particular passages. As the continuous preacher brings these things to expression, the congregation has opportunity to build on interpretation from week to week.

Does Not Allow the Preacher to Flinch

Preaching from a biblical book from start to finish does not allow the preacher to flinch when the preacher encounters a difficult text. As noted elsewhere, a text may be hard to understand, especially given the cultural distance from antiquity to today. A text may also raise theological and ethical difficulties for the congregation. Coming upon such texts, preachers are often inclined to pass by on the other side of the road. But when the preacher has made a commitment to preach through a biblical book, the sermon must deal with the problematic issues.

Saves Preparation Time

Continuous preaching can save preparation time. A preacher should always take account of the historical setting of a book, its literary features and function, and its theological claims. When jumping from text to text from week to week to week, however, the preacher must redo these tasks each week. The minister traversing a single book does not have to make a new beginning in these things every seven days, but builds up a reservoir of information about the background of the biblical book from which the preacher can draw from one Sunday to the next. The preacher can then have more preparation time for thinking hermeneutically and homiletically. The sermon, like tea in the cup, may develop depth as it steeps.

Of course, *continua* preachers need to be sure they keep fresh. While familiarity can create the conditions for deeper exploration of the text, it can also become an excuse for sloughing off or getting stale.

Things to Keep in Mind

While continuous preaching has an impressive pedigree and a trustworthy set of recommendations, such preaching does not automatically mean the congregation will engage the sermon. This section brings out several things the preacher might keep in mind to help the congregation enter (and stay in) the world of the sermon. The other side of nearly all of these positive suggestions is a point at which continuous preaching can take a bad turn. Like many other starting points in preaching, the dangers of *lectio continua* are often as much in the preacher's practice as in the approach itself.

Choose Biblical Material Pertinent to the Congregation

Preachers who do not follow the lectionary can choose any of the books of the Bible (or parts of books) for continuous exposition. Preachers committed to the lectionary have a smaller universe of possibilities for semicontinuous and continuous preaching. Either way, the preacher must choose which biblical material (if any) to follow continuously. A danger here is that the preacher can choose biblical material that does not connect in a life-giving way with the congregation.

There are many reasons for focusing on a particular biblical book, all under the umbrella of lifting up biblical material that has a good chance of helping the congregation make theological sense of God and the world. A preacher ought to make such a choice critically, aware of what the congregation gets and loses with each choice.

On the one hand, a typical approach is for the preacher to look for a biblical book written for a historical situation similar to that of the congregation. A congregation's particular biblical or theological anemia may call for the congregation to become better acquainted with a particular body of biblical literature. A preacher may turn to a book whose themes fit into themes in the congregation's life. On the other hand, a contemporary congregation might benefit from a sustained encounter with a biblical community in a very different situation.

From time to time, a preacher may choose a particular biblical book mostly because the preacher is fascinated with the material. A preacher's energy for a book is sometimes enough to generate interest in the congregation, at least for a time.

Occasionally, preachers decide to preach continuously through the entire Bible from start to finish. For them, the reason for preaching from Judges is that it comes after Joshua and before Ruth. Other preachers view the Bible as a kind of grab bag: a minister can pull out any biblical book and preach from it.

Keep the Sermon Lively and Connected to Today

Every sermon needs to be lively enough to invite the congregation's participation in it. I lift up this quality in regard to preaching *lectio continua* along with its accompanying danger: *continua* preachers sometimes become so absorbed in details of ancient history, culture, and literary analysis that the sermon becomes more an informational lecture than a real conversation with the text and the congregation. A preacher who excelled in close reading of the text in an upper-level Bible class in theological school may be tempted to continue that practice from the beginning to the end of the sermon.

The congregation's interest in a sermon can be crushed by the weight of too much information presented with too little attention to its significance or without a theological frame of reference or connection to today. Preaching *lectio continua* calls for the preacher to find ways of interweaving historical and contemporary connections (historical, literary, and theological) so the congregation can ascertain what the text asked the congregation in antiquity to believe and do as a way of helping today's community think about what it can believe and do.

Maintain a Balance between the Big Picture and the Details of the Text

When preaching continuously, the preacher needs to maintain a balance between keeping the big picture of the biblical material before the congregation while also honoring the details of the text for that day. With regard to the latter, apropos of an earlier remark, the sermon should help the congregation understand both how the big picture illumines our understanding of the individual passage and how the individual passage contributes to the big picture. The interplay is sometimes a prime starting point for the sermon.

The weight of this comment falls on keeping the big picture in mind. The twin faces of danger here are (a) the preacher focusing on the big picture so much that sermons sound the same week after week or (b) focusing on the details so much that the sermons are essentially disconnected. The first time I preached through a book of the Bible (five sermons on Philippians), I really offered five individual sermons on texts from Philippians rather than a systematic exposition of the book. With little effort, I could have tied the sermons together so they functioned in thematic coherence with one another and with Philippians as a whole.

Slice the Biblical Material into Bite-Size Chunks

Preachers and scholars of preaching sometimes say that television has reduced the attention span of the typical congregant to about the length of a segment of a television show—three to five minutes, seven tops. Some theoreticians even propose structuring the sermon in such segments. This approach is reductionistic. People can be involved in communication events for much longer when a genuine interaction takes place between speaker and listeners. When it comes to attention span and worship, my observation is that people are socialized toward particular lengths of time. However, even when the Bible reading and sermon interact with the congregation's search for meaning, the congregation has a limit to its attention span.

The preacher, then, needs to slice the book of the Bible into chunks that are bite-size, according to the congregation's appetite. The danger is that a sermon running too long often leaves the listening community bloated and more relieved that the sermon is over than strengthened by participating in it. The brevity of some sermons can itself become distracting. For some congregations, a single passage and a ten-to twelve-minute sermon is a meal. For other congregations, both the length of the passage and the length of the message can be much longer.

Be Sensitive to How Long the Congregation Can Sustain Interest in One Book

Just as the preacher needs to slice the material into bite-size chunks for each Sunday, so the preacher needs to preach on a biblical book for the number of weeks a congregation can continue to converse seriously with the material. I write as if the continuous preacher would normally start at the beginning and work through the biblical material to the end. Some congregations would welcome this approach with any book in the Bible. I read recently about a minister who has been preaching from Romans for three years and has another two years to go. Evidently this minister's congregation is at home with such a protracted approach. However, the listening ability of some congregations, especially in the long-established churches, would be exhausted by complete *continua* through some books of the Bible if the sermons stretch into too many weeks, months, or (gulp) years. A danger, obviously, is that the congregation can grow weary of the continuing movement through the biblical material.

My sense is that some congregations in the historic denominations and movements are ready for a month or six weeks on a single book, others for eight to twelve weeks, with only a few congregations prepared for sustained attention to a single book over several months. Many (not all) evangelical congregations are already accustomed to hearing sermons on a single body of biblical material over many months. Preachers can help socialize congregations into prolonged conversations with biblical books.

Keep Listeners Up to Date and Orient Newcomers

While a core of listeners are in worship every week, people do miss. To help folks who missed last week get the context for this week's biblical material, the congregation needs to provide updates on the progress of the preaching. New people come into the congregation in the middle of preaching through a book. A similar set of strategies can both keep people on board who have missed and can introduce newcomers to the progress of the series.

A preacher could create a flow-line showing the starting and ending points of the continuous preaching and marking individual sermons along the time. A timeline is often ideal for narrative texts. A linear summary of the unfolding of the material would work well with nonnarrative texts, such as the prophetic literature and the Letters. The preacher can provide such summaries in a simple chart form. Whatever instrument the preacher uses, the effect is to help the congregation recognize where they are in the ongoing biblical material.

The flow-line could indicate the Sundays on which the sermons are scheduled and the relevant biblical passages. The timeline would be particularly inviting if the preacher could paint the sermons in provocative strokes. The content of the timeline might raise existentially important questions and pose ideas that arrest the congregation's attention. A graphic artist might illustrate the overview. This material could be posted in the worship bulletin, on the big screen, on the church website, on the Facebook page, and in other public faces of the congregation. The preacher can also provide a quick and easy-to-read summary of the message from the previous week in a short teaching moment in connection with the reading of the scripture lesson.

Preview What Comes Next

My spouse and I almost never watch television. However, we are hooked on the series *Downton Abbey.* At the end of each broadcast, the preview of the coming episode sparks our desire to watch the next episode. We want to be part of what comes next. In a similar way, the preacher can preview material for the next week or weeks. The preview could be included in the sermon itself, or in a brief preview moment at the end of the service, or, as previously stated, in the worship bulletin, on the big screen, on the website or the Facebook page, or in other public formats.

Change Text and Focus When the Occasion Calls for It

The preacher needs to be ready to change the text and focus of the sermon when circumstances arise that can be better addressed from a different text or theological perspective than the one(s) coming up in the biblical material. As in the case of preaching from the *Revised Common Lectionary*, the preacher may be surprised at how well the preselected biblical material fits emerging situations. But when that is not the case, preacher and congregation should take a break from the planned material and turn to more salient resources.

Preaching Semi-Continuously

While preaching continuously from start to finish may be the ideal for most biblical books, circumstances (such as the congregation's limited attention span) may preclude long periods of time dwelling on one book.[8] Ministers might then preach semi-continuously through biblical materials. The semi-continuous minister does not preach from every passage in the biblical material but chooses a limited number of texts from which to work. The semi-continuous pattern gives the preacher the opportunity to acquaint the congregation with the main features of a large body of biblical material in a relatively short period of time.

Select Truly Representative Texts

Semi-continuous preaching imposes an important responsibility on preachers: to select texts that truly represent the larger document. Some passages are hubs around which other parts of the letter turn. These texts lift up ideas that put the congregation in touch with the big picture within the document. When an essential text is left out, the continuous effort in preaching is compromised.

As an example of semi-continuous preaching, here is an overview of sermons from Judges, a book included only once in the lectionary. As the book begins, God lifts up the judges as agents whose dramatic actions bring about renewal. As the book unfolds, judges themselves become increasingly disobedient until, at the end, the community is in chaos. The book epitomizes the deuteronomic contention that obedience brings blessing and disobedience invokes curse. Along the way, texts in Judges raise several hornet's nests of theological questions with respect to God using or authorizing violence to bring about the divine will.

1. Judges 2:1-4, 11-22: the unfaithful situation in the land after Israel had occupied it.

2. Judges 4:1-24: God uses obedient Deborah to save the community of Sisera. (Deborah represents faithful judges of Judg. 3:7–5:31.)

3. Judges 6:1–8:35:[9] Although God uses Gideon to save the community from the Midianites, Gideon is only partially obedient, eventually engaging in idolatry. (Gideon represents judges who are both faithful and unfaithful in Judg. 6:1–10:17.)

4. Judges 11:1-40: Jephthah makes a promise: if God will deliver the community from the Ammonites, Jephthah will sacrifice the first person to come from his house. That person turns out to be his own daughter. (Jepthah represents judges who slide toward disobedience in Judg. 11:1–12:15.)

5. Judges 13:1–16:31: Samson saves the people from the Philistines but violates God's desires by falling in love with Delilah, a Philistine woman, and falls under judgment. (Samson represents the further slide of judges toward disobedience in Judg. 13:1–16:31.)

6. Judges 20:1–21:25. Unfaithfulness leads to civil war and the near destruction of the community. (This text represents the results of disobedience in Judg. 17:1–21:25.)

Among other things, the book of Judges gives the preacher a platform to reflect with the congregation on the degree to which leadership in communities (especially within the church) and the leadership of communities themselves points toward possibilities for blessing or possibilities for curse.

Pay Attention to the Semi-Continuous Selections in the Revised Common Lectionary

The preacher working with *lectio continua* in the *Revised Common Lectionary* needs to look carefully at the appointed lections. By and large, the semi-continuous assignments in the *Revised Common Lectionary* are good representatives of the documents from which they are taken. This is largely true, for instance, in the lectionary's partition of Romans. However, once in a while the lectionary leaves out important material, as for instance, when the lectionary omits Romans 1:18-32, with its turgid analysis of gentile sin. That passage is utterly foundational for understanding the book of Romans.

Paul wants gentiles to understand what God has done for them and how that should bring them into mutually supportive relationship with Jewish believers.

Preaching through Sections within Books of the Bible

Some sections within books of the Bible are excellent candidates for continuous preaching. In this case, the preacher does not work through the entire book, but takes a continuous approach to the part that is most meaningful at the time of preaching.

When taking this tack, the preacher needs to help the congregation understand the place of the section in the book as a whole. Sermons and other expository materials should provide an overview of the historical, literary, and theological background of the book and the purposes of the book in its ancient contexts. Of course, the pastor should help the congregation understand the purpose of the section within the larger biblical work. For example, a pastor might preach continuously through Isaiah's "little apocalypse" (Isa. 24–27) or through the Sermon on the Mount (Matt. 5–7). A preacher needs to guard against treating the section in isolation from its context in the book.

Preaching continuously is an old and honored approach. While a preacher needs to be careful while following *lectio continua*, it has tremendous power to help congregations today enlarge their biblical and theological literacy as well as their sense of mission.

CHAPTER 5

Preaching from the African American Lectionary and Other Cultural and Civic Calendars

When preachers from long-established churches of European origin use the phrase "the lectionary" in conversation among themselves, they usually mean the *Revised Common Lectionary*. The question, "Do you preach from the lectionary?" typically means, "Do you preach from the *Revised Common Lectionary*?" However, the word *lectionary* by itself refers in a general way to any organized pattern of readings. The *Revised Common Lectionary* is only one lectionary. Moreover, a lectionary is only one way of organizing a congregation's preaching calendar. We have already noticed that a minister can preach from the Christian year without using a lectionary. Some churches and communities follow calendars that coordinate with their own culture and history.

This chapter first looks at the African American Lectionary, a lectionary replete with resources for preaching and worship gaining strength in many African American congregations. We turn next to the possibility that churches in other cultures might use the African American Lectionary as a model. We pause over civic calendars as a starting point for preaching, and end by calling attention to some ways churches supplement the *Revised Common Lectionary*.

The African American Lectionary

While quite a few congregations in the African American community follow the Christian Year and the *Revised Common Lectionary*, a growing number of African American congregations are taking up the African

American Lectionary.[1] The African American Lectionary began publication in 2007 under the leadership of Martha Simmons.[2] The lectionary itself was given its form by a large body of scholars and ministers with a wide breadth of acquaintance with the African American church.

In one way, the African American Lectionary is new (having begun its formal life in 2007). In another way, many themes in the African American Lectionary are quite old, as this lectionary brings together days and emphases, including major holy days also found in the Christian year, that have been important to many African American congregations. For example, many African American congregations have long honored the Pastor's Anniversary and the Ushers and Nurses Guild Day. The African American Lectionary also introduces new days and themes, such as LGBT Sunday, Anti-Incarceration Sunday, and Entrepreneurship Sunday.

An aim of this lectionary is to help congregations highlight the "joy, freedom, and challenges of being both African Americans and Christian."[3] Many of the emphases in this lectionary are unique to African American religious culture while others are distinctive of that culture without being entirely unique to it. Some congregations follow the emphases of the lectionary every week. Other churches combine the days and texts of the African American Lectionary with free selection of preaching material, local plan, or occasional elements of the Christian year and the *Revised Common Lectionary*. Its creators hope that "the African American Online Lectionary allows users to select from a vast array of material that will exactly fit their congregation's needs and expectations."

Days of the Lectionary Year

The African American Lectionary contains about sixty events and emphases. Most of these days are just that: specific Sundays. But some elements of the calendar are seasons (for example, Lent), while others, such as the Spring and Fall Revivals include days of the week in addition to Sunday. Here are the days of the African American Lectionary in a recent year in the approximate order in which they occur. I say "approximate" because some days and seasons, such as Lent, move from year to year. Congregations sometimes add days, such as Church Officer's Installation Day, or omit days in the following calendar.

Emancipation Day and Juneteenth
Health Day
Dr. Martin Luther King Jr.'s Birthday (Beloved Community Day)

Economic Justice/Financial Literacy Sunday
A Celebration of Black History
Marriage Enrichment Sunday
Ash Wednesday
Season of Lent
African Heritage Sunday
Women's Day (March is Women's History Month)
Church Anniversary
Children's Day (Birth–Age 12) (Literacy)
Palm Sunday
Holy Thursday
Good Friday
Easter
Youth Day (ages 13–17) (Literacy)
Spring Revival
Pastor's Anniversary
Earth Day
Anti-Addiction Day
Mission Sunday (Mission Work Abroad)
Mother's Day
Pentecost Sunday
Christian Education Sunday/Graduation Sunday
Restoring the Peace (Community Action Day)
Ushers and Nurses Guild Day
Father's Day
LGBT Sunday
Stewardship Sunday
Generations Day
Entrepreneurship Sunday
Anti-Incarceration/Social Justice Sunday
Anti–Domestic Violence Sunday
A Service of Healing (For those suffering emotional distress, grief, divorce, and physical ailments)
Young Adult Sunday
Evangelism Sunday
Singles Sunday
Celebration of Vocations Day (Labor Day)
Seniors, Elders, and Grandparents Day
Homecoming/Family and Friends Day
Worship and Arts Sunday

Fall Revival
Youth Sunday (Ages 13–17) (Building Self-Esteem)
"Who So Ever Will" Sunday
Children's Sunday (Birth–Age 12) (Building Self-Esteem)
Men's Day
Celebrating Our Saints Day
Ecumenism Sunday (Different Faiths Worshipping Together)
Thanksgiving
First Sunday of Advent/World Aids Day
Second Sunday of Advent
Third Sunday of Advent
Fourth Sunday of Advent
Christmas
Kwanza
Watch Night

Resources to Support the African American Lectionary

In addition to listing days for the church year along with appropriate biblical materials, the African American Online Lectionary provides three kinds of resources for every day of the lectionary year for the preacher and other worship planners: Lectionary Commentary, Cultural Resource, and Worship Resource. These resources are written by recognized scholars and ministers. A different person writes for each week. The writers add their own touches to their contributions, so these descriptions are representative.

Lectionary commentary. The lectionary commentary usually begins with a historical and contemporary description of the liturgical moment. The commentator offers an extensive interpretation of the biblical material for the day, which includes attention to the contemporary context and social location as well as more traditional exposition of the biblical text. The writer focuses on elements of celebration, descriptive details, sounds, sights, and smells. Suggestions for the sermon include an outline that fully develops certain parts of the sermon.

Cultural resource. The writer for the cultural resource section indicates the historical significance of the day, followed by the writer's own autobiographical connection to the day in which the writer recounts her or his personal experience of the day. A biographical reflection lifts up the story of individuals or groups whose lives have had a particular connection to the day or to its emphases. Commentators tend to include songs that speak to the moment, a memorable learning moment, and resources for learning more about the moment.

Worship resource. The worship resources vary from week to week in accord with the nature of the Sunday and the kinds of things that are available. Worship resources, again developed by a recognized figure, often include litanies, hymns and congregational songs, spirituals and traditional songs, and gospel songs for choirs and praise teams. However, liturgical dance, anthems, modern songs, and instrumental pieces for the offertory and for the period of prayer are also used. The worship resource often concludes with musical suggestions to accompany the sermon, for the invitation to discipleship, and for the close of the service. This section includes sources for all selections and pertinent copyright information.

The framers of the African American Lectionary wisely note that while these resources are often widely applicable, particular congregations and preachers must judge whether the resources for a given week fit the particular context of the congregation.

Gains with the African American Lectionary

As a person of European origin, I hesitantly offer critical reflection on the African American Lectionary. These remarks originate from my own social location, from observation of African American congregations, and from interaction with ministers and students from such congregations. These critical reflections should themselves be the subject of critical reflection.

Addresses Identity and Context

One of the most far-reaching themes in all aspects of contemporary ministry and congregational life—biblical interpretation, theology, ethics, mission, education, pastoral care, pastoral leadership, worship, and preaching—is the importance of honoring the context of ministry. The African American Lectionary speaks directly to African American contexts. It takes account of issues that are urgent in the African American context. It draws on resources from African American (and broader pan-African) traditions, history, figures, events, and concerns. It educates the community. It empowers African-American identity, reinforces the respect due all human beings, and nurtures pride. The African American Lectionary communicates that African American individuals and communities have power and agency in North American culture still dominated by Eurocentrism and racism. It equips individuals, households, and groups with the perspectives and skills necessary to maintain a strong sense of cultural and communal life, to operate within the dominant culture, and to take steps toward changing that culture.

Facilitates Mutual Interpretation

The African American Lectionary facilitates mutual interpretation between African American culture and interpretation and other interpretations of Christian tradition. Of course, there is no such thing as pure Christian tradition. This tradition is always expressed through a particular interpretation. In North America, Eurocentric churches typically represent their interpretations of Christian tradition as Christian tradition itself when they should more honestly and perceptively identify their interpretations as their interpretations. From this perspective, the African American Lectionary helps the African American Church articulate an interpretation of Christian tradition that is genuinely African American.

At the same time, this lectionary encourages mutuality of interpretation that prompts the church to be open to points at which the Bible and voices in Christian tradition from within and beyond the African and African American contexts can help the African American church think afresh about God's presence and leading. While the African American Lectionary privileges African American perspectives, sources, and writers, it recognizes that African Americans do not have a monopoly on wisdom, and encourages preachers to be open to insight wherever it is found.

Connects the African American Church to the Broader Spectrum of Churches

I have already alluded to this strength. While the African American Lectionary focuses on African American church and culture, it seeks to connect the African American Church to the broader spectrum of churches. It does so in two ways. First, its lectionary year is anchored in days and practices that are shared by nearly all Christian communities—Ash Wednesday, Lent, Palm Sunday, Holy Thursday, Good Friday, Easter, Pentecost Sunday, Celebrating Our Saints Day, Thanksgiving, the Sundays of Advent, and Christmas. Second, it focuses on additional days that are observed in wider North American culture or churches, such as Martin Luther King Jr.'s Birthday (Beloved Community Day), Mother's Day, Father's Day, and Celebration of Vocations Day (Labor Day). The African American Lectionary specifically calls for Ecumenism Sunday as a day for different churches and religious groups to worship together.

Emphasizes Mission

The Christian year and the *Revised Common Lectionary* assure the congregation of redemption by telling the story of Christ. While a persistent emphasis in Ordinary Time is growing in discipleship, which includes growing in witness and mission, the Christian year and the RCL do not expressly emphasize the importance of engaging in mission. To be sure, the African American Lectionary assures the congregation of God's redeeming presence and activity.

Planning and Availability of Interpretive Resources

The African American Lectionary helps the preacher and worship leaders with planning and resources. Biblical materials, theological themes, cultural connections, resources for worship—all are available long in advance. Moreover, the preacher can easily set aside the African American Lectionary when something happens in the congregation or in the larger world that calls for the preacher's attention.

Provides a Venue for Other Groups to Express Solidarity

While the African American Lectionary is designed for use in African American Churches, ministers and congregations from other cultural settings could profit in two ways from becoming familiar with the African American Lectionary and the resources that accompany it. First, the African American Lectionary would help people from other communities become acquainted with certain aspects of African American churches and concerns important to African American communities. Such outreach could be in the spirit of Ecumenism Sunday in the African American Lectionary, whose goals include developing mutual awareness and solidarity among different communities of faith.

Second, the African American Lectionary might inspire clergy and congregations in other settings to ponder aspects of their own cultures that could be represented in the ecclesial calendar they follow. Of course, when members of communities outside the African American church approach the African American Lectionary in these ways, they should do so in a spirit of respect and solidarity, and not as ecclesial and cultural voyeurs.

Cautions with the African American Lectionary

The potential cautions that come to this reviewer's mind with respect to the African American Lectionary are only that: potential cautions. Although they seem logical to me, they come from the outside looking in. I am sure factors that escape my perception are at work. Nevertheless, for the sake of my own integrity and, perhaps, for the sake of promoting conversation, I record these reservations.

The Congregation May Not Hear the Sweep of the Biblical Narrative

While the African American Lectionary presumes that biblical material will be at the center of each Sunday service, this lectionary does not presently give the congregation an opportunity to hear the sweep of the biblical narrative (or the larger Christian story). Our similar reservation regarding the *Revised Common Lectionary* need not be repeated here.[4] But it is worth noting that a preacher and congregation could easily depart from the African American Lectionary for a while and tell the biblical story through an African American lens.

Needing a Comprehensive Picture of the Christian Faith

Christian faith assumes that the congregation will come to clear convictions regarding what it believes about God, Christ, the Holy Spirit, God's purposes in both present and future worlds, the church, and other matters. The African American Lectionary provides resources for thinking about these matters, but not in a systematic framework that goes week by week in helping the congregation work its way through basic questions and issues. The Christian year and the *Revised Common Lectionary* do not do this either. In my view, from time to time preachers need to depart from these overarching plans for preaching and develop sermon series that help congregations make systematic and (reasonably) comprehensive articulation of what they most deeply believe.[5]

The African American Lectionary as Model

While the preaching in many congregations with racial-ethnic foci takes account of the particular cultural settings of the congregations, as far as I know, the African American church is the only North American community with a racial-ethnic focus to develop a lectionary comprehensively keyed to its particular culture. To be sure, racial-ethnic churches often lift up particular days and emphases important to their cultures.

Diversity is one of the permeating emphases of the emerging post-modern ethos in North America. One wonders if the time is ripe for churches associated with other racial and ethnic communities to follow the lead of the African American Lectionary and to develop lectionaries and broader approaches to ecclesial life that are specific to their cultures.

Such an effort might begin with people in a particular culture identifying qualities, like the following, that could then be worked into a calendar and lectionary:

- Formative events in the history of the community and its culture

- Important figures and their contributions

- Traditions that carry the community's ongoing identity

- Values at the core of the culture

- Practices that shape the life of the community

- Issues faced by individuals and communities, especially issues that the church should address

- Points at which the Bible, Christian tradition, doctrine, and practice reinforce the community and its culture

- Points at which the Bible, Christian tradition, doctrine and practice challenge the community and its culture

- Points at which the culture reinforces elements of the Bible, Christian tradition, doctrine, and practice

- Points at which the culture challenges elements of the Bible, Christian tradition, doctrine, and practice.

With such material in hand, and with a working knowledge of the Bible and theology, a church in a particular culture can formulate a lectionary that helps the church engage in mutual critical correlation between the culture and Christian identity so that a church can be truly enculturated while not being captivated by the culture.

Eurocentric Churches and the Model of the African American Lectionary

It might be an illuminating exercise for churches of European origin to name the issues that seem most pressing to them. A glance at the African American Lectionary reveals a number of issues that are important to that community, for example, economic justice, the state of marriage, literacy, the care of the earth, addictions, community action, LGBT concerns, incarceration, domestic violence, the single life, caregiving, and HIV/AIDS. The African American Lectionary leads the church to reflect on these issues from the perspective of Christian faith. A Eurocentric church might name the issues that are similarly important both in the immediate existential level and at the deeper systemic (and sometimes hidden) level. To what degree is a church of European background actually addressing its pressing issues in theologically meaningful ways? Such a church might create a liturgical calendar for a year, or for part of a year that follows the lead of the African American Lectionary in naming and setting aside times to focus on such concerns.

In any event, Eurocentric culture is not entirely a monolith. Churches from particular European backgrounds often set aside days for saints or other figures or events important to their homelands or histories. Bridget of Sweden, for instance, is sometimes lifted up in Lutheran churches of Swedish background. While working on this chapter, I was reminded that congregations with a Welsh background sometimes observe St. David's Day. A congregation with a name such as John Knox Presbyterian Church typically remembers days and themes associated with the Scottish reformer, such as Knox's birthday or death day. I once served as a student in a Presbyterian church of Scottish heritage that honored the birthday (and poetry) of Robert Burns.

Twin Dangers

Twin dangers accompany this effort. One is that a church can use its culture, with its values and practices, to co-opt Christian tradition in such a way that the latter simply serves the former without making critical adjustments. The church may be tempted to use Christian trappings to bless a cultural heritage without genuine mutual interpretation. Indeed, cultural

86

values can sometimes serve as blinders that prevent a church from seeing things that it needs to see.

One of the most horrific examples of such a phenomenon in the United States is the way in which churches in the South in the early 1800s used particular interpretations of the Bible and Christian theology to justify slavery. When slavery was formally ended, similar interpretive moves were made in support of segregation and other forms of racial oppression that continue to this very day. While this case may be extreme, it underlines the fact that churches cannot unreflectively celebrate efforts to bring together cultural mores and behaviors and Christian vision.

The other danger is that elements in the church—especially churches of Eurocentric origin—can equate their own cultural background with core concerns of Christian faith and can then attempt to get people in other settings to abandon their own cultures and to live according to Western cultural conventions. This classic case in this regard, of course, is missionaries from churches of European origin imposing Western cultural values on converts in other parts of the world during the massive missionary movements of the late 1800s and early 1900s. Less perniciously, perhaps, but nevertheless in the same stream of phenomena is churches today—Western and otherwise—who assume that their interpretation of Christian faith is the norm for understanding and enacting Christian faith.

When traveling this path, the church needs to be engaged in persistent critical theological reflection. Indeed, such reflection should be part of the church's travel on any path.

Preaching and the Civic Calendar

As we observed in the introduction, throughout much of twentieth century, and in some corners of the church today, quite a few congregations organized their worship and preaching around the civic calendar amalgamated with key dates in the Christian calendar. In the congregation in which I grew up, for example, our preaching and worship included Sundays of preparation for Easter (though we did not call them Lent), Palm Sunday, Maundy Thursday, Good Friday, Easter, World Communion Sunday, and Sundays of preparation for Christmas (though we did not call them Advent). In addition, we focused on Washington's Birthday and Lincoln's Birthday (when they were observed separately prior to the consolidation of President's Day), Mother's Day, Memorial Day, Children's Day, Father's Day, Fourth of July (Freedom and Democracy Sunday), Labor Day, and Thanksgiving, At some point we added Race Relations Sunday.

87

Preachers and scholars of preaching often bemoan the ways in which focusing on the civic calendar can erase the line between the church and the culture. Flag-waving, jingoism, sentimentality—these are just some of the critiques levied against some of the preaching that accompanies a civic calendar. Indeed, I myself have elsewhere described a good many churches in this mode as "high priests of culture" who saw their mission as propping up Eurocentric middle-class mores and property values.[6]

However, misuse does not mean that preaching in relationship to the civic calendar is inherently unfaithful. If the fundamental purpose of preaching is to help the congregation name God's presence and purposes and to respond accordingly, then the preacher could enact that purpose in relationship to the civic calendar by raising the question, "How does the emphasis in public life associated with a particular civic day compare and contrast to the purpose of God?" On the Fourth of July, for instance, the preacher does not have to wave the flag in an uncritical way but can help the congregation reflect on not only the ways in which national life is consistent with the purposes of God but also the ways in which that life is contrary to God's aims.

Supplementing the *Revised Common Lectionary*

Our review of the histories of development of both the Christian year and the *Revised Common Lectionary* in chapters 1, 2, and 3 emphasized that God did not personally inscribe these approaches to ecclesial life on tablets of stone. The church created them in order to help the Christian community maintain a living faith and make a vital witness. In view of changing circumstances, then, the church can modify these things to help strengthen faith and empower witness. Toward this end, I call attention to three efforts to supplement the Christian year and the *Revised Common Lectionary*. These efforts conclude that while the Christian year and the RCL have many useful elements, their value can be increased by slight reshaping or additions.

A Season of Creation

More than fifty years ago, A. A. McArthur proposed a season of creation as part of the Christian year, but churches did not find it compelling.[7] Recently, aware of increasing tensions between humankind and nature, and mindful of the solidarity that should exist between humankind and nature, a fresh approach by three leading biblical scholars—Norman Habel, David Rhoads, and H. Paul Santmire—calls for a Season of Creation.[8] The creators envision the season being observed between September 1 and St. Francis Day (October 4), a time when the fecundity of the earth is often visible through the harvest. It can also take place at other appropriate times of the year.

The proposal acknowledges that nature is a living entity with whom the human family lives (or should live) in covenant, and envisions the congregation worshiping with nature. The writers unfold the theology of this season by imagining several of its elements as a service of worship:

Opening prayer: a God of all creation
Invitation and Gloria: kinship with creation
Confession of sin: alienation from creation and reconciliation
Scripture: listening to creation (and listening to what human beings say about creation)
Proclamation: incarnation (Jesus' role in creation, and Jesus belonging to the earth) and reconciliation
Offering: creation as gift
Sacraments: Jesus' presence (Jesus present in the sacraments as a sign of how Jesus is present in all creation)
Commission and blessing: the church's mission to the earth.

The authors also call attention to the human bias in the church's tradition of interpreting biblical and theological material related to nature. They urge contemporary Christians (and others) to identify with the earth, to retrieve the voices of creation, to discern the restorative powers of the earth, to see the interrelationship of human justice and ecological justice, and to find Christ at work throughout.

Based on this interweaving of theological themes, the authors set aside four Sundays each year as a season of creation.

Year A: the focus is on the Spirit and creation.
    First Sunday in Creation: Forest Sunday
    Second Sunday in Creation: Land Sunday
    Third Sunday in Creation: Wilderness Sunday
    Fourth Sunday in Creation: River Sunday
Year B: the focus is on the word and creation.
    First Sunday in Creation: Earth Sunday
    Second Sunday in Creation: Humanity Sunday
    Third Sunday in Creation: Sky Sunday
    Fourth Sunday in Creation: Mountain Sunday
Year C: the focus is on wisdom and creation.
    First Sunday in Creation: Ocean Sunday

Second Sunday in Creation: Fauna Sunday
Third Sunday in Creation: Storm Sunday
Fourth Sunday in Creation: Cosmos Sunday

Following the pattern of the *Revised Common Lectionary*, four scripture readings are appointed for each Sunday: a first reading from the Torah, Prophets, and Writings; a psalm; a second reading from an epistle; and a reading from a Gospel.

Year D: Readings Not Found in the Current Lectionary

Timothy Slemmons, who teaches at the University of Dubuque Theological Seminary, laments that important slices of biblical material are not found in the *Revised Common Lectionary*. To help bring these omitted passages into congregational consciousness, he proposes a "principle of canonical comprehensiveness" to foster representation of a wider selection of biblical material.[9] Professor Slemmons thus formulates Year D, a fourth year to add to the current lectionary. For each Sunday, Year D proposes four readings on the model of the *Revised Common Lectionary*: a first reading from the Torah, Prophets, and Writings; a psalm; a second reading from an epistle; and a reading from a Gospel.

As the foregoing analysis would predict, Year D is largely made up of lections not found in the current lectionary. Whenever possible, the assigned passages lean toward continuous reading. This addendum gives greater emphasis to the Torah, Prophets, and Writings than does the RCL.

Year D looks at the familiar texts in the two major cycles from fresh angles.[10] The first major cycle—Advent–Christmas–Epiphany Day—will have the most familiar feel to the regular lectionary user. While the texts are new, they are chosen according to similar patterns in the RCL. The second major cycle—Lent–Easter–Pentecost Day—will feel at home to the regular lectionary user through Easter. On the Sundays after Easter, Year D makes a significant improvement over the *Revised Common Lectionary* by including a reading from the Torah, Prophets, and Writings, whereas the RCL drops that reading and replaces it with one from Acts.

The biggest changes in structure in Year D come on the Sundays of Ordinary Time after Pentecost Day. The readings begin with six weeks (the ninth Sunday of Ordinary Time through the Fourteenth Sunday) from the Gospels, focusing on important themes in Jesus' ministry (exorcisms, parables, some teachings). Beginning with the Fifteenth Sunday of Ordinary Time, the readings in Year D focus on the last days of Jesus' ministry: the end-time discourse (Fifteenth through Nineteenth); confrontations in Jerusalem (Twentieth through Twenty-Third); and the arrest, trial, suffering, and death of Jesus (Twenty-Fourth through Thirty-Third).

Holy Days of Justice

As noted in chapter 3, the *Revised Common Lectionary* is sometimes criticized for downplaying the prominent place accorded to justice in the Bible. A recent commentary on the RCL takes two steps toward remedying this situation.[11] The first is to offer an interpretation of every lection in the lectionary from the perspective of social justice. The second is to introduce twenty-two new Holy Days for Justice. Some of these days commemorate events that are quite painful. They are called "holy" not because they are happy but because God has a particular concern for them. The days are as follows:

World Aids Day (December 1)
Universal Declaration of Human Rights (December 10)
Martin Luther King Day (January 15)
Asian American Heritage Day (February 19)
International Women's Day (March 8)
Salt March Day (Marching with the Poor) (March 12)
Oscar Romero of the Americas Day (March 24)
César Chavez Day (March 31)
Earth Day (April 22)
Holocaust Remembrance Day: Yom haShoah (27th of Nissan, usually
    from early April to early May)
Peace in the Home: Shalom Bayit (second Sunday in May)
Juneteenth: Let Freedom Ring (June 19)
Gifts of Sexuality and Gender (June 29)
Fourth of July: Seeking Liberty and Justice for All (July 4)
Sojourner Truth Day (August 18)
Simchat Torah: Joy of the Torah (mid-September to early October)
International Day of Prayer and Witness for Peace (September 21)
Peoples Native to the Americas Day (fourth Sunday in September)
World Communion Sunday (first Sunday in October)
Night of Power (27th Night of Ramadan: From 2011 through 2020 the
    date moves from September to August, July, June, May, and April)
World Food Day (October 16)
Children's Sabbaths (third weekend in October, or another date that
    works for the congregation)

The Holy Days for Justice are distributed approximately equally throughout the year. A preacher and congregation can substitute the readings and focus of a Holy Day for Justice for the regular focus and readings in the *Revised Common Lectionary*. As for the season of creation and Year D, the same types of readings are appointed for the Holy Days for Justice as for the days in the RCL: a reading from the Torah, Prophets, and Writings; a psalm; a reading from a letter; and a reading from the Gospels.

CHAPTER 6

Preaching from the Chronology of the Bible and from Schools of Thought within the Bible

When I want to get to know someone in depth, I often ask him to tell me his life story: where he grew up, what that place was like, significant things that happened from then until now, how he reacted at the time, and how those things play into what he thinks and does today. I want to know her formative relationships, experiences, ideas, feelings, values, choices, and activities. I try to ask why he responded as he did to certain events, why they took particular turns, what they learned along the way, and what he might do differently. I want to know how a person perceives how the ways in which the things that happened to her in the past shape who she is and why she acts as she does in the present.

Postmodern interpreters remind us that we do not have pure and objective perception. We do not tell our stories in a scientific fashion. A story is always told from a certain point of view. Hearing the story usually reveals that point of view, how it functions for the person, and why it is important to the storytelling community.

The Bible is an important part of Christian identity. At this point, I thought about saying, "The preacher needs to help the congregation learn and interpret the biblical story if we are to understand who we are and how we are to act." At one level, this statement is true. The biblical materials all share certain points of view. But the catch is the article "the" in the phrase "*the* biblical story." While there is an overarching canonical story, the specific materials in the Bible are diverse. Not only is the Bible itself diverse, but preachers also interpret the Bible in diverse ways.[1] As a friend said, the Bible is less a book and more a library. The preacher needs to help the congregation become critically acquainted with the points of view the biblical materials have in common and with the diverse points of view among the different theological families in the Bible. Each theological household has its own story.

This chapter looks at three ways of preaching that help a congregation become acquainted with major biblical stories. The first is to preach through the formative events and ideas of the Bible. The preacher chooses texts from Genesis through Revelation that summarize the overarching biblical story. The second is to tell the stories of the major theological families in the Bible—Yahwist, Elohist, Deuteronomistic, priestly, wisdom, end time (apocalypticism), and Hellenistic Judaism. The third is to help the congregation recognize how the final form of the biblical materials addressed the situations for which they were given that form.

Preaching the Overarching Biblical Story

As I point out in chapter 2, the *Revised Common Lectionary* never presents the sweep of the biblical story in one continuous narrative. Nevertheless, it is imperative for the congregation to have a sense of the sweep of the biblical story. For one thing, as pointed out in the introduction, the Bible contains the formative story of the church and offers the earliest interpretations of who we are and what we are to do. For another thing, awareness of the Bible as an overarching story gives the congregation a framework within which to place individual Bible readings.

While materials in the Bible represent considerable theological diversity, the Bible as we have it is presented as an overarching story from the beginning of history in Genesis to its climax in Revelation. True, as we said at the outset of the chapter, the diversity of biblical material reminds us that the story can be interpreted in different ways. At the same time, these materials share some common themes. Furthermore, the story of Jesus makes fullest sense only within the larger story of Israel, which itself only makes fullest sense within the yet larger story of creation.

Long ago, James A. Sanders proposed that the church develop a table of readings that follows the overarching story told in the Bible.[2] The minister chooses passages that represent the formative events and ideas of the Bible and preaches sequentially on those texts from Genesis through Revelation. The preacher chooses the number of texts and weeks according to listening ethos in the congregation. The attention span of some congregations will be exhausted in twelve weeks. Others will be ready for a year or two or three.

A Sample Table of Readings

This sample table of readings follows the major eras in the unfolding story of Israel: from creation through the story of Israel to Jesus and his earliest followers to the climax of history in the book of Revelation. To mirror the approximate proportions of the two testaments in the Bible, this table of readings contains thirty-seven readings from the Torah, Prophets, and Writings and fifteen from the Gospels and Letters.

Creation and Fall
1. The God of Israel is the creator of the world: Genesis 1:1–2:4

2. The disobedience of the first human beings brings about the fall: Genesis 3:1-22

3. Disobedience magnifies to the point that God destroys the whole earth: Genesis 6:1-8; 7:17-24; 8:6-7, 20-27; 9:8-17

4. After the unified human community transgresses at Babel, God divides the human family into separate groups: Genesis 11:1-9

Sarah and Abraham and Ancestral Stories
5. Call of Sarah and Abraham and covenant with them as God's plan to bless all peoples: Genesis 12:1-9; 15:1-21

6. Isaac: Genesis 22:1-19

7. Jacob and Esau: Genesis 22:29-45; 33:1-17

8. Joseph: Genesis 37:1-24; 45:1-15

Exodus, Covenant at Sinai, and Wandering in the Wilderness
9. Egypt enslaves the Hebrews, but God calls Moses as God's agent in freeing them: Exodus 3:1-15

10. God delivers the Hebrews from slavery: Exodus 15:1-17

11. God makes covenant with the Hebrews at Sinai: Exodus 20:1-20

12. The people wander in the wilderness because they disobeyed, but God sustains them: Numbers 11:1-15

Entry into the Promised Land
13. As God promised, the people cross into the land: Joshua 3:1-17

14. God delivers Jericho (a case study in God fulfilling the divine promises): 6:1-25

Life under the Judges

15. Deborah sings of victory: Judges 5:1-30

16. Samson illustrates the unfaithfulness that beset the judges and the community: Judges 16:4-22

Rise of the Monarchy

17. Israel requests a monarch: 1 Samuel 8:1-22

18. Samuel anoints Saul as first ruler of Israel: 1 Samuel 9:27–10:8

19. God makes covenant with David: 2 Samuel 7:1-17

20. Solomon builds the first temple: 1 Kings 8:22-32

Divided into Two Nations

21. The one state divides into two nations: 2 Kings 17:7-41

22. Amos prophesies judgment to Israel (the northern nation): Amos 5:10-14

23. Hosea prophesies restoration to Israel: Hosea 11:1-11

24. First Isaiah prophesies judgment on Judah (the southern nation): Isaiah 5:1-30

25. Micah prophesies restoration to Judah: Micah 4:1-13

Exile in Babylonia

26. The exiles weep beside the waters of Babylon: Psalm 137

27. Jeremiah gives pastoral guidance to exiles: Jeremiah 29:1-23

28. Ezekiel calls the community to distinguish between true and false shepherds: Ezekiel 34:1-30

29. Second Isaiah promises God will return the exiles to the homeland: Isaiah 43:1-21

Return to the Land as a Colony of Persia

30. Haggai encourages a community dispirited because the restoration of their life takes longer than expected: Haggai 1:1-15

31. Ezra calls the community to obedience as the path to renewal: Nehemiah 8:1-12

Psalms and Wisdom
32. Community laments give voice to grief: Psalm 44

33. Individual psalms of thanksgiving express gratitude for deliverance: Psalm 116

34. Enthronement psalms honor God as sovereign of the universe: Psalm 97

35. Lady wisdom calls from the street: Proverbs 1:20-33

36. Job objects to a popular Deuteronmistic notion that obedience and disobedience result in blessing or curse: Job 1:1-22; 4:1-11; 16:6-17

Rise of End-Time Thinking (Apocalypticism)
37. Jewish life in the Hellenistic age is difficult, giving rise to end-time (apocalyptic) hope: Daniel 7:1-14

Ministry of Jesus
38. Jesus is born as God's agent to announce the coming of the Realm and to prepare people for it: Luke 1:39-56

39. Jesus preaches and teaches the realm of God: Matthew 4:12-22; 7:21-27

40. Jesus demonstrates the realm of God through table fellowship and miracles: Mark 3:13-17; 5:24b-34

41. Jesus is crucified by the Romans as a threat to the peace: Mark 14:43-50; 15:6-15, 33-39.

42. God raises Jesus from the dead and places Jesus at God's right hand: Luke 24:1-12; Acts 1:1-11

Life of the Early Church
43. The coming of the Spirit shapes the life of the community: Acts 2:1-21, 42-47

44. The community witnesses with power but encounters opposition: Acts 3:1-10; 4:1-22.

Ministry of Paul
45. God calls Paul as apostle to the gentiles: Galatians 1:11-24

46. For Paul, the church is grafted into the mission of Israel: Romans 11:11-32

47. The church is to embody the Realm in its community life: Romans 12:9-21

97

48. Paul hopes to live in the Realm after the second coming: 1 Corinthians 15:35-57

Ministry of Others in the Late First Century
49. Paul's disciples struggle with how to relate to the culture: women in the community as an unfortunate case study: 1 Timothy 2:8-15

50. Members of the church sometimes suffer because of their witness: 1 Peter 3:8-22

51. The church needs to endure: Hebrews 12:1-13

Climax of History
52. The church anticipates a new heaven and new earth after the second coming: Revelation 21:9–22:5

To reduce the series, a preacher might select just one text from each category. To extend the series for two, three, or more years, a preacher could expand the number of texts in proportion to each section.

Tips for the Trail

What follows are some tips that can help honor the otherness of the biblical materials and to engage the congregation. Many of the suggestions and cautions mentioned in connection with continuous preaching also apply here.

Focus on the Era, Not Just on the Specific Passage

When preaching from the overarching story of Israel, the preacher should focus on the era. What were the issues and questions facing Israel or the church in each era? What did the biblical writers see as God's purposes in each era? The preacher should not simply preach from the texts cited in the preceding outline, but use the texts as points of entry into the larger net of things the congregation needs to know.

Christmas and Easter

Every time I suggest this approach to clergy, the first question is, "What do we do about Christmas and Easter?" The simplest response is to depart from this sequence on the Sundays around Christmas and Easter and to preach from traditional Christmas and Easter passages. If the preacher wanted to hit fifty-two Sundays of preaching exactly (forty-eight Sundays following the Bible and two Sundays each on Christmas and Easter), the preacher would subtract some texts from the list and replace them with texts associated with Christmas, and texts associated with Palm/Passion Sunday and Easter. A creative and daring pastor could launch the chronological sequence on the first Sunday of the year (or some other starting point) and use the texts that appear in the chronology of the Bible at the time of Christmas and Easter as the preaching texts, making appropriate links to Christmas and Easter themes.

Provide a Timeline

Preaching chronologically through the Bible invites the use of a timeline marking the Sundays and the sequence of texts. A timeline visually reminds the congregation of its location in the biblical chronology. As in the case of the flow-line discussed in the previous chapter in connection with continuous preaching, a timeline could be mounted in the worship space, projected on the big screen, included in the worship bulletin, or placed on the congregation's website, Facebook page, newsletter, and other public spaces.

Teaching Moments and Summaries

To help the community locate the text and the era it represents in the life of Israel, the preacher might add a short teaching moment to the reading of the Scripture lesson to furnish the congregation with information about the era of Israel's life that is the subject of the day. The preacher could also provide data either orally or on the big screen about the era that does not fit into the sermon.

The preacher could provide summaries of the congregation's progress through the Bible that both rehearse where the congregation has been and point to where the congregation is going. These summaries could appear in the newsletter, the website, the Facebook page, and other modes of communication.

Use Visual Materials

Preaching chronologically through the Bible invites the use of visual materials. Maps can help the congregation locate where events took place. The preacher can also project drawings and photographs of artifacts and places that coordinate with the sermon, such as drawings of the first, second, and third temples; photographs of archaeological artifacts; photographs of places like Mount Sinai and the Jordan River; and charts that show the relationship of people, drawings, and photographs of scenes associated with texts, such as vineyards or sheep.

99

Telling the Stories of the Theological Families That Shaped the Bible

The preacher and congregation are in a peculiar situation with regard to the biblical story and the writing (and purposes) of the biblical books. The Bible appears to tell a story that goes from creation in Genesis through the life of Israel, the ministry of Jesus, and the witness of the early church to the coming of an entirely new world in the book of Revelation. Without doubt many books of the Bible contain reminiscences of the actual history described in the biblical book(s) telling that story.

Yet, many of the biblical books were given their present form long after the events described within those books took place. The later writers reshaped the earlier traditions in order to speak to their later times. For example, although the story of Sarah and Abraham probably took place about 1800 BCE, the priestly theologians gave the story its present form at the exile (597–533 BCE). These theologians wanted the exiles to identify with Sarah and Abraham, and to hear the story of the ancestral couple as the story of God's promise to the exiles. As God made good on the promises to Sarah and Abraham, so God would make good on the promises to the exiles.

From this point of view, the congregation ideally should know not only the great arc of the biblical narrative but also when, why, and how the major theological families gave the texts their present form in relationship to that arc. Indeed, biblical materials in their present format often tell us more about the theological families that shaped them than they tell us about the characters and events narrated in the materials.[3]

I now briefly describe the seven primary theological families in the Bible and list representative biblical materials from those families. These households are Yahwist, Elohist, Deuteronomistic, priestly, wisdom, end-time theology (apocalypticism), and Hellenistic Judaism.[4] A time chart in the next section depicts the emergence of these families in relationship to events in the life of the people.

A preacher can look at any text through the lens of its theological family. In addition, I recommend that the preacher offer sermons specifically designed to introduce the congregation to these theological households. These theological groups are like family members in the congregation's extended family tree. The preacher might develop a series of seven sermons, one on each family, using a representative text (or texts) from each family. Or the preacher could develop a series of sermons on each theological family using texts from the body of biblical material associated with that family. Along the way, the preacher can help the congregation think about how it resembles and differs from the various theological households in the Bible.

100

Prior to the Yahwist

Israel had a tradition, sometimes called *Israel's national epic,* prior to the Yahwist. This theological tradition probably contained earlier forms of stories of creation, the ancestors (Sarah and Abraham; Jacob, Leah, and Rachel; Isaac and Rebekah; and Joseph), and the exodus from Egypt.[5] This epic, which climaxed in the Mosaic covenant, explained the origins of the world, Israel's identity and vocation, formative aspects of Israel's history, how Israel differed from other peoples, and the faithfulness required for Israel to maintain the blessing of God. Prior to the Yahwist, Israel entered the Promised Land and lived as a loose confederacy under the Judges. The Yahwistic, Elohistic, priestly, and Deuteronomistic schools of thought reinterpreted this epic by reshaping the actual details of the narrative to make it fit their purposes.[6]

Yahwist

The name Yahwist comes from the preference of these writers for the name *Yahweh* (translated "the Lord") for God. The Yahwists are often dated about 950 BCE.[7] The tribal confederacy under the judges had given way to the united monarchy. Israel was now a nation alongside other nations. The Yahwists interpreted the national epic so as to claim that the united monarchy was God's purpose. The Yahwist viewed God as sovereign of all history, who would guide the new state of Israel in its relationships with other peoples. God called Abraham and Sarah to become the means whereby all nations of the earth received blessing. God raised up the monarchy as the means whereby Israel would itself become a great nation so that other nations would look to the way of Israel as the way to blessing.

Some representative Yahwistic texts: Genesis 2:4b-25; 3:1-24; 4:1-16; 6:1-4; 6–9 (contains some priestly material); 11:1-9; 12:1–13:18; 16; 18–19; 24; 26; 29; 34; 37–50 (contains some Elohist and priestly material); Exodus 1–17 (contains some Elohist and priestly material); Numbers 13–14 and 16 (both contain some priestly material).

Elohist

The name Elohist comes from the preference of these writers for the name *Elohim* (translated "God") for God. The Elohists began writing about 850 BCE after the division of the united nation into two smaller ones—Judah in the south and Israel in the north.[8] The Elohist interpreted Israel's epic to justify the existence of the northern nation as a distinct state. The Elohist gives greater priority to the covenant with Moses than to the monarchy. This writer speaks often of the "fear of God" in the old-fashioned sense: the Elohist's God is so powerful the community should be fearful of disobeying this God.

Some representative Elohistic texts: Genesis 20:1-18; 22:1-10, 16b-19; 32:22-32; 37–50 (includes some Yahwist material); Exodus 1:15-21; 3:1-15 (includes Yahwist material); 13; 17–18; 19:1-9; 10:1-17 (includes some priestly material); 20:18–23:33; 24:1-18 (includes priestly material); 32–33; Numbers 11–12; 22–24; and Psalms 42–83 (Elohistic psalms).

Deuteronomistic Theology

The Deuteronomists began to formulate their theology about 650 BCE. It developed over the next century and was likely given its present form during the exile. The heart of the Deuteronomistic tradition is a simple set of assertions.[9] God has made covenant with Israel. The purpose of the covenant is blessing. The covenant contains guidelines (commandments) for the way to blessing. When the community is obedient, blessing follows. When the community is disobedient, curse follows. The curse is not an end in itself but is to awaken the community to the need to repent—to turn away from disobedience and to turn toward obedience and blessing. According to the Deuteronomistic viewpoint, God made an everlasting covenant with David (2 Sam. 7:1-16).

The Deuteronomists did not create this theological framework as a matter of abstract theological speculation. These thinkers sought to explain that the nation had collapsed because the nation's rulers and people disobeyed the terms of the covenant through such things as idolatry, exploiting the poor, miscarrying justice, and entering improper foreign alliances. The exile was the definitive curse. Repentance would be the path to national renewal. The Deuteronomistic school saw the future of Israel beyond exile as a renewed monarchy featuring obedience to the Deuteronomistic theology.

Some representative texts: Deuteronomy, Joshua, Judges, 1 and 2 Samuel, 1 and 2 Kings, Jeremiah, Lamentations, Amos, Hosea, Micah, Nahum, Habakkuk, Zephaniah.

Priestly Writers

The priestly theological writings began to surface by 550 BCE. Whereas the Deuteronomistic writers saw the future of Israel after the exile as a renewed monarchy, the priestly theologians envisioned the reorganization as a theocracy in which God ruled through the priests and community worship.[10] Beginning by prefacing their theological reconstruction of the national epic with the majestic poem of Genesis 1, the priests portrayed God as creator and sovereign who graciously keeps covenant with all (Gen. 9:1-17) and who, through covenant with Sarah and Abraham (Gen. 17:1-14), called Israel to the special work of witnessing to the way of blessing to other human families. At Sinai God revealed the commandments as the qualities of life that lead to communal blessing.

While some of the distinctive characteristics of the life of Israel seem strange to people today—such as circumcision, sacrifice, and dietary practices—the priests believed that God intended such things to help Israel maintain its distinctive identity in the face of acculturation and other threats. The second Isaiah envisions the restoration of all human families (Isa. 45:22). One of the most enduring priestly achievements was to edit the Torah (Genesis, Exodus, Leviticus, Numbers, and Deuteronomy) and other materials from the priestly perspective while allowing for the different points of view of the Yahwists, Elohists, and Deuteronomistic writers to remain recognizable.

Some representative texts: Genesis, Exodus, Leviticus, Numbers, 1 and 2 Chronicles, Ezra, Nehemiah, Isaiah 1–39, Isaiah 40–55, Ezekiel, Haggai, Zechariah 1–8, Joel, Malachi.

Wisdom

The wisdom literature is hardest to date and describe because it originated at different times for many different purposes and exists in many different genres.[11] Generally speaking, the sages believe that we learn about God's purposes by reflecting on experience. The wisdom teachers emphasize quite different things. The proverbs typically offer commonsense observations on God's purposes and how to live in harmony with them. Ecclesiastes questions the degree to which life has meaning. Job challenges the Deuteronomistic theology that obedience always brings material blessing and disobedience always brings curse.

Some representative texts: Job, Proverbs, Ecclesiastes, and wisdom psalms.

End-Time (Apocalyptic)

Fully developed end-time theology came to expression in response to conditions in Israel in the Hellenistic age (roughly 300 BCE to 200 CE).[12] During this period, Israel was almost constantly a nation under foreign occupation. The end-time thinkers constructed a theology of history designed to help their communities recognize the limited authority of the occupying nations and to encourage Jewish communities to endure in the midst of occupation, suffering, and even persecution. This theology holds that God has divided history into four ages: (1) the idyllic life in Eden; (2) the fall;

(3) the broken old age, which includes the present period of history, marked by Satan and the demons and by idolatry, exploitation, sickness, scarcity, violence, and death; and (4) the coming realm of God, the end-time, which will be much like Eden (the beginning time), marked by the rule of God in every circumstance and characterized by love, joy, health, abundance, peace, and everlasting life. God will end the old and begin the new by means of an apocalypse when God destroys the old world and replaces it with a new one.

Some representative texts: Isaiah 56–66 (proto-apocalyptic), Zechariah 9–14 (proto-apocalyptic), Daniel 7–12, Matthew, Mark, Luke, Acts, Romans, 1 and 2 Corinthians, Galatians, Ephesians, Philippians, Colossians, 1 and 2 Thessalonians, 1 and 2 Timothy, Titus, Philemon, James, 1 and 2 Peter, Jude, Revelation.

Hellenistic Judaism

While end-time thinking was one response to the Hellenization, Hellenistic Judaism was another. Whereas the apocalyptic thinkers largely rejected all things Hellenistic, some Jewish theologians sought to bridge Jewish tradition with Hellenistic influences (including Greek philosophy) by interpreting Jewish thought in light of Greek categories and vice versa. Of most interest to the biblical preacher is a modified form of Plato's two-story universe in the background of such writings.[13] In these terms, heaven (a sphere of life, light, truth, freedom, and abundance) is the upper story, and the world is the lower one (a sphere of death, darkness, lying, slavery, and scarcity). While human beings live in the lower story during the earthly life, God makes it possible to journey to the upper story at death.

Some representative texts: Gospel of John; 1, 2, and 3 John; and Hebrews. This thinking makes occasional appearances in the Letters. Some materials not found in the Protestant canon exhibit some qualities of this strain: Philo, Wisdom of Solomon, Sirach (also known as Ben Sira or Ecclesiasticus), and 4 Maccabees.

Preaching from Biblical Writings in the Order They Emerged

The first part of this chapter suggests acquainting the congregation with chronology of the biblical story as the Bible tells it from creation to the new heaven and new earth. The chapter closes with a suggestion that is a riff on both that discussion and on the immediately preceding discussion of preaching from the theological families in the Bible. The suggestion now is to preach from biblical writings in the order in which they came to their present form and to do so from the perspective of the theological families that gave them that form.

Such sermons would help the congregation discover the order in which the biblical materials came into being and the purpose of the biblical materials in their contexts. The preacher would not so much tell the story *within* the text as tell the story *of the situation to which the text was addressed and how the biblical writers shaped their version of the story* to affect the congregation in that situation.

Following is a time table correlating significant events in the history of biblical times with specific biblical texts. The pastor could preach sequentially from the beginning of the table to the end, or, more likely, the pastor could preach from representative eras and texts, the number of sermons depending on the attention span of the congregation.

Ministers could make extensive use of the same aids mentioned in connection with preaching from the chronology of the Bible: timeline, teaching moments and summaries, updates, and visual aids. Such supportive efforts might be especially important if the congregation is unaccustomed to thinking about the relationship of the biblical documents to history in this way.

From Sarah and Abraham through the Monarchy

Approximate date	Ruler, event, or situation faced by the community	Biblical material addressing event or situation
1800–1700 BCE	Sarah and Abraham, and other ancestors	
1700–1600	Ancestral family goes to Egypt	
1600–1300	In Egypt	
1300–1200	Exodus from Egypt	Exodus 15:21 (Song of Miriam) (the oldest piece of literature in the Bible)
1200–1020	Life under the judges as loose tribal confederacy	Materials that become Israel's national epic come to expression
1020–922	United monarchy: Saul, David, Solomon, building of the first temple	Yahwist begins to interpret the united monarchy as God's plan
922	The united nation divides into two: Israel in the north (922–721) and Judah in the south (922–587)	

The One State Divides into Two Nations

Date in Israel (North)	Ruler, event, or, situation in Israel	Biblical material addressing situation in Israel		Date in Judah (South)	Ruler, event, or, situation in Judah	Biblical material addressing situation in Judah
922–901	Jeroboam I	After 922, Elohist begins to interpret emergence of Israel		922–915	Rehoboam	
876–869	Omri: founding of Samaria			873–849	Jehoshaphat	
869–850	Ahab	Elijah prophesies				
849–842	Jehoram			849–842	Jehoram	
842–815	Jehu			837–800	Jehoash	
786–746	Jeroboam II	Amos prophesies (proto-Deutero-nomistic)		783–742	Uzziah	Hosea prophesies (proto-Deutero-nomistic)
735–722	War between Aram and Israel	First Isaiah begins to prophesy (proto-priestly)				
721	Fall of Samaria					

Events Leading to the Exile and the Exile

Date (in Judah)	Ruler, event, or situation faced by the community	Biblical material addressing situation
715–687	Hezekiah	Micah prophesies (proto-priestly)
	701: Siege of Jerusalem	First Isaiah's second period of prophecy (proto-priestly)
640–609	Josiah	
		Zephaniah prophesies (628–622) (proto-priestly) Nahum prophesies (proto-priestly)
		Jeremiah's first period of prophecy (626–621) (Deuteronomistic)
621	Deuteronomistic reform	Early form of Deuteronomy and perhaps early form of Deuteronomistic history
609–587	Jehoiakim	Habakkuk prophecies (605) (proto-priestly)
	597 First deportation of exiles to Babylon	Jeremiah's second period of prophecy (Deuteronomistic)
593–587	Zedekiah	Jeremiah's third period of prophecy (Deuteronomistic)
		Ezekiel's first period of prophecy (priestly)
587	Jehoiachin Fall of Jerusalem	
593	Second deportation to Babylon	
587–538	In exile in Babylon	Deuteronomistic theology given form in which we know it: Deuteronomy, Joshua, Judges, 1 and 2 Samuel, 1 and 2 Kings.

107

Date (in Judah)	Ruler, event, or situation faced by the community	Biblical material addressing situation
587–538, continued	In exile in Babylon, continued	Lamentations (Deuteronomistic)
		Ezekiel's second period of prophecy (priestly)
		Second Isaiah prophecies (Isa. 40–55) (priestly)
		Priestly theology becomes forceful in shaping Genesis, Exodus, Leviticus, Numbers. Priestly theology influences several subsequent prophets.

Return from Exile and Living as Colony of Persia, Subsequently Occupied by Other Foreign Powers

Date	Ruler, event, or situation faced by the community	Biblical material addressing the situation or community
539	Cyrus the Persian defeats Babylon	
538	Edict of Cyrus makes it possible for exiles to return to homeland	
538–519	Judah (Yehud) becomes colony of Persia Many exiles return home	Third Isaiah begins to prophesy (Isa. 56–66) (priestly/proto-apocalyptic)
	520 Begin rebuilding the temple	Haggai (priestly) Zechariah 1–8 (priestly)
	515 Dedication of the second temple	
460	Continuing life as colony of Persia	Malachi (priestly)
450–430		Ezra and Nehemiah (Deuteronomistic)

Date	Ruler, event, or situation faced by the community	Biblical material addressing the situation or community
400s		Jonah Job (Wisdom)
333–323	Alexander the Great conquers much of the Mediterranean basin: begins policy of Hellenization which continues for five centuries	Zechariah 9–14 (priestly/proto-apocalyptic)
323–200	Life under Egyptian occupation	
300s		Psalms collected as we know them, voicing a variety of theological families
		Joel (priestly) 1 and 2 Chronicles (priestly)
200s 250		Proverbs (Wisdom) Song of Solomon (Wisdom) Ecclesiastes (Wisdom)
200–168	Life under Syrian (Seleucid) occupation	
170		Esther
168–165	Maccabean Revolt	Daniel 7–12 (apocalyptic)
	Judah is self-governing for about 100 years	

Jesus and the Early Church under Roman Occupation

Date	Ruler, event, or situation faced by the community	Biblical material addressing event or community
63 BCE	Rome conquers Jerusalem Roman occupation begins	
4 BCE	Jesus is likely born[14]	
27–30 CE	John the Baptist Ministry of Jesus	
30	Death, resurrection, and ascension of Jesus	
30ff	Pentecost and life and witness of early community	
33–35	Paul is called as apostle to gentiles	
33–64	Ministry of Paul	
49–51		Paul writes 1 Thessalonians (apocalyptic)
50–58	Paul writes each book to a congregation with its own situation by bringing an end-time perspective to bear on each congregation.	Paul writes: Galatians (apocalyptic) 1 and 2 Corinthians (apocalyptic) Philippians (apocalyptic) Philemon (apocalyptic) Romans (apocalyptic)
61–64		Paul dies in Rome
65–75		One of Paul's students writes Colossians (apocalyptic with Hellenist Jewish touch)

Date	Ruler, event, or situation faced by the community	Biblical material addressing event or community
70	Romans conquer Jerusalem and destroy the temple; tensions within Judaism and within the church as well as between some Jewish leaders and some congregations. Many questions enervate both groups: Why did the temple fall? What is our future? Who is truly faithful to the Jewish heritage?	Gospel of Mark (apocalyptic)
80–90	Each of the rest of the books in the Gospels and Letters was written to particular congregations with particular issues. Writers interpret the situations of each congregation from the perspective of their theological family.	Matthew (apocalyptic) Luke-Acts (apocalyptic) 1 Peter (apocalyptic) James (apocalyptic) Ephesians (apocalyptic) Jude (apocalyptic)
90–100		Gospel of John (Hellenistic Judaism) 2 Thessalonians (apocalyptic 2 Peter (apocalyptic) Revelation (apocalyptic) Hebrews (Hellenistic Judaism
100–110		1 and 2 Timothy and Titus (apocalyptic) 1, 2, and 3 John (Hellenistic Judaism)

CHAPTER 7

Preaching a Series That Starts with the Bible

On the first day of Introduction to Preaching, I ask students to name some things about which they are anxious in regard to their preaching ministries. Someone nearly always says, "Will I have enough to say? Will I be able to fill up twenty minutes every week?" Encountering students years later, conversation inevitably turns to preaching, as in, "Do you remember how I was concerned about whether I would be able to fill up twenty minutes every week? Just the opposite. I have more to say than I can fit into a sermon. Some issues are just too big for one twenty-minute message."

Because some subjects are too big for one sermon, a preacher may want to turn to a sermon series. The following are the usual starting points for developing a series:

- Biblical materials

- Christian doctrine

- Christian practice

- Issues related to the congregation

- Issues related to personal life

- Issues related to the social world (including nature)

- Some mix of these.

Something catches the preacher's attention, and the preacher concludes that the subject matter is important enough to develop a series around it.

This chapter deals with series whose point of origin is conversation with the Bible. The preacher begins with something in the Bible and moves to today. Preachers can also start sermon series from Christian doctrines, Christian practices, and personal and social issues. These latter possibilities come up in chapter 8.

This chapter begins by describing sermon series, then raises the question of when to preach in a series, and finally, highlights some things the preacher can do to help the congregation engage the series. After considering the ups and downs of preaching in a series, we look at sample ways of developing sermon series that begin with the Bible: series in which sermons build on one another, series on different interpretive perspectives in the Bible, and series on biblical characters. These examples are only that: examples of the many different ways a preacher may develop a series.[1] The chapter ends with a list of representative possibilities for sermon series.

When to Preach in a Series?

In a sermon series, a preacher puts together a sequence of sermons that explore a common subject in more depth and breadth than a single sermon can do. While each sermon should be a complete message, the effect of the series is cumulative. An analogy: a student at seminary can benefit from an individual class session in systematic theology, but being in class for every session in the semester can help the student place the topic of that one session in the wider perspective of the class as a whole.

When a Subject is Bigger Than a Single Sermon

The most obvious reason for developing a series is to explore a particular subject in more depth and detail than is possible in a single sermon. A series allows preacher and congregation to spread the treatment of the subject over the length of the series. For example, many people in the United States presently ponder the meaning of marriage. A sermon series would give the preacher the opportunity to explore the different forms of marriage in the Bible—one man and one woman, a man and several wives, a man and wife with concubines, levirate marriage (a man marrying his brother's widow), and the possibility of marriage between people of the same sex.

Pastoral Listening: The Key to Formulating a Sermon Series

The key to selecting a focus for a series is pastoral listening. At one level, the preacher should attend to what the congregation explicitly says they want. At another level, the preacher needs to listen to the story behind the story, that is, to the larger network of experiences, issues, ideas, and relations that is going on (or not going on) in the congregation and in the wider world about which the congregation needs greater theological clarity or missional direction. The congregation often has semiconscious or unconscious needs that should be addressed in order to help the community mature in faith and witness. Through pastoral listening, a preacher can become aware of points at which the congregation needs a deeper exploration of an aspect of the Bible than the preacher can develop in a single sermon, or matters related to personal life, household life, congregational life, and beyond.

While a series typically emerges from a minister's pastoral listening, the preacher's personal interest in the subject matter is sometimes enough to power a series, as long as the series connects with the world of the congregation. Preachers may feel so claimed by a subject that they just have to preach on it. Preachers may be deeply concerned about a subject. Preachers may come face-to-face with questions they need to explore. When such an impulse seizes the preacher's imagination, the preacher should pause and reflect critically on whether the moment is right in the congregation's life for the preacher to follow that impulse.

Multiple Ways to Organize a Series

A sermon series can be organized in many different ways. Preachers can select a model of organization that serves the purposes of a particular series. Over time, a preacher could employ several different patterns of organization. I mention five easy-to-use patterns of structuring series and one that is more imaginative and challenging.

Laying Bricks

The most common model is laying bricks. In the same way that a brick mason creates a wall by laying bricks side by side and then builds row upon row, the preacher builds one sermon upon another. Week after week, the sermons add to one another.

Look at the Subject from Different Perspectives

A preacher can look at the subject from different perspectives. A model here might be a conversation in which people from different places are involved. We are all talking about a common subject, but Eurocentric people in the Midwest of the United States see it differently from folk who live in Maine, who see it differently from the delegation from the South Sahara, who see it still differently from those who live in Hong Kong, whose perspective is different yet from North Koreans.

Telephoto Lens: Enlarging or Contracting

A preacher could organize the series along the lines of using a telephoto lens. From sermon to sermon the view of the subject expands. The first sermon might deal with the implications for the individual, the second for the household, the third for the congregation, the fourth for the municipality, the fifth for the nation, and the sixth for the world. The reverse can also be true: just as a skilled photographer can adjust the telephoto lens from wide angle to narrow, so the preacher could move from world to nation, municipality, congregation, household, and individual.

Stating the Reasons for a Viewpoint

Having been a member of debate teams in high school and college, I always want to know the reasons for things. A series gives the preacher an opportunity to develop reasons for a position advocated by the preacher, congregation, or denomination. The preacher reasons for the position advocated in the series as a whole. The preacher could devote one sermon to each of the several important reasons for a position.

Pieces of a Jigsaw Puzzle

One of the most imaginative and challenging ways of organizing a series is to think of each sermon as a piece of a jigsaw puzzle and to assemble the sermons in a series in a way similar to putting together the pieces of a jigsaw puzzle. The full point of view in this series would come into view only as the series ends. This approach is quite challenging, as it depends both upon the congregation to trust the preacher with some residual uncertainty from week to week and upon the congregation to have the mental acuity to keep the pieces in place from one Sunday to the next.

This pattern may work best in a week of preaching when the congregation is coming together each night for worship and preaching for several nights. One of my teachers, Neill Hamilton, did this in chapel. While a graduate student in Switzerland, he became a mountain climber. Each day in chapel for a week he told the story of part of a climb, leaving us hanging as to what would happen next. Only on Friday, in the context of a service of the loaf and the cup, did he—and we—reach the top of the mountain and the point of the series.

Things to Keep in Mind When Preaching in a Series

There are several things a preacher needs to keep in mind when developing a sermon series, whether it is originating from the Bible or elsewhere. Some of these qualities are similar to what preachers should generally keep in mind but are refracted through the particular concerns of the sermon series.

Connect with the Congregation

First, the series needs to interact with the situation of the congregation. It needs to make a meaningful connection with folk. Typically the preacher focuses a series around needs, issues, or questions (whether perceived or not) in the congregation. Such series typically take wing and fly. The preacher does need to pay particular attention to the congregation's engagement with series that comes more from the preacher's own energy for the subject than from the preacher's pastoral listening to the congregation.

Develop a Real Series

A series needs to be a real series; that is, the sermons need genuinely to relate with one another. A preacher should not put together a bunch of texts and subjects that are only peripherally related and call them a series. The latter approach not only erodes the congregation's trust in the preacher but also calls into question the preacher's intellectual capability.

Each Sermon Has a Complete Message

Each sermon needs to stand on its own. While the sermons in the series must mutually support one another, for the sake of listeners who will not hear the entire series, each week the sermon needs to communicate a distinct message, even if the message is incomplete from the perspective of the series as a whole.

Help the Congregation Track the Series

As mentioned in the previous chapter, for the sake of congregants who miss some Sundays in the series as well as for those who attend regularly but lose track of the series, the preacher should help the congregation keep the big picture of the series in mind by describing the series and by alerting the congregation to where a particular sermon fits into the series. A description and a sermon series timeline can be posted on the website, on Facebook, in the newsletter, in the worship bulletin, in newspaper advertising, in radio and television spots, and in other means through which the congregation makes its life known in the public arena.

Create a Sense of Anticipation

When a series is engaging, listeners look forward to the next service of worship in a way similar to viewers anticipating the next episode of a favorite television series. When preaching in a series, a preacher and worship leaders have the advantage of being able to plan in advance what we named in connection with the Christian year, the lectionary, continuous preaching, and preaching through the chronology of the Bible.

Keep the Sermons at a Reasonable Length

Preachers need to keep the series at a length congenial to the congregation's attention span. Congregations in the old-line denominations are likely to be comfortable with series that last four to eight weeks. Many congregations, particularly in other wings of the church, may be socialized into much longer time frames.

Pull the Plug if Necessary

If the series starts but then dies on its feet, the preacher needs to consider reshaping it or abandoning it. Preachers sometimes misread a congregation's level of interest or misperceive some other aspect of the preaching ethos that impacts the ability or willingness of the congregation to follow the series.

In such cases, the better part of wisdom may be to kiss the series good-bye in a gracious way.

Sample Sermon Series

We turn now to several examples of sermon series whose points of origin are in the Bible. Let me stress that these are only examples. The number of possible sermon series sparked by the Bible is limited only by the number of Sundays available for preaching in a minister's lifetime.

A Series in Which the Sermons Build on One Another

Many biblical writers, however, like authors of short stories and novels today, develop ideas, meanings, and characters over the length of the document. Indeed, a key insight from literary criticism and philosophy of art is that the experience of a document in its own medium is a part of the meaning of that document to the reader. A narrative is intended to be heard or read so the reader experiences the unfolding of the narrative in the reader's imagination. While a preacher can extrapolate propositions and ideas from the story, the propositions and ideas are almost always less than the fullness of hearing and experiencing the story.

By contrast, a sermon series gives a preacher an ideal opportunity to lift up key texts that illumine the theme of the series. Indeed, a preacher can offer the congregation optimum insight by focusing not just on one passage but on the theme as it emerges across the document. Progress from text to text as the preacher moves from sermon to sermon allows the congregation to experience the unfolding of the series.

A series in which sermons build on one another can come from a single biblical book (such as the example series from Second Isaiah proposed below). It can also come from several books by the same author or theological family, such as the letters of Paul or the priestly writings. Or such a series could follow a theme across several different books from different times and places, especially when biblical writers intentionally echo particular themes from biblical books other than the ones they wrote.

An Example: The Servant Songs in Second Isaiah. The prophet we often call Second Isaiah or Deutero-Isaiah (Isa. 40–55) spoke during the exile to reassure the exiles that God, creator and sovereign of the earth and all its inhabitants, would liberate the community from exile and return them to their homeland. As sovereign of all, God was concerned not just about Israel but also about the other peoples of the world. Echoing the priestly point of

119

view, the prophet interpreted God not only as intending homecoming for Israel but as remembering God's promises to Sarah and Abraham to bless all peoples through them and their heirs. For Second Isaiah, this blessing includes justice: the nations will learn how to live so that all in the community can live in peace, mutual support, and shared abundance.

The prophet, then, must explain how a people in exile can be a means of blessing for other more powerful nations. A key part of Isaiah's answer is that God can use Israel's situation as an example to other peoples. As God's servant, Israel continues to trust in God's promises even when the community is taken into captivity. Israel continues to trust in God both for its own deliverance and for God's blessing to come to the other nations even when Israel suffers. When God redeems Israel, the great and powerful nations will see that the God of Israel is truly God of all and will heed the vision of justice that Israel embodies.

The prophet portrays the aforementioned mission of Israel in a series of four songs that are spread across Second Isaiah's prophecy. In a sermon series on these songs, each sermon would build on the previous one until reaching the climax in the most famous of the songs.

1. First song: Isaiah 42:1-9 (The life of the servant community points to justice for all.)

2. Second song: Isaiah 49:1-7 (The life of the servant community is a light—a model—to the nations.)

3. Third song: Isaiah 50:4-11 (Although the servant community appears to be put to shame, God will vindicate the community.)

4. Fourth song: Isaiah 52:13–53:12 (The most famous of the servant songs: God will use the faithfulness of Israel in the midst of suffering as a testimony to other peoples of the world; others will recognize God in the movement toward redemption and justice among all peoples.)

This series would be an ideal path to Easter, as the preacher could place the suffering and resurrection of Jesus in this tradition

A Series on Different Perspectives in the Bible

A preacher can easily put together a series organized around different perspectives on a particular subject in the Bible. While this approach can serve the congregation anytime, it is especially useful when a congregation is struggling with a particular issue that has a resonance in the Bible. By listening to different perspectives in the Bible, the congregation encounters a series of others who offer the perspectives that the congregation can take into account as it moves toward its own sense of theological conviction about the subject. This approach is also useful when the congregation has developed an unhealthy rigidity, because this approach helps the community recognize a plurality of points of view within the Bible itself. This series models a conversational theological method: the people listen to different viewpoints in the Bible with an ear toward coming to their own perspective on the focal matter.

The preacher would clarify the focus of the series. Each sermon would lift up a different point of view. In each message, the preacher could indicate what each perspective offers the congregations as well as the limitations of that point of view. Along the way, the preacher can compare and contrast the distinct viewpoints.

Example: A Series on Different Interpretations of Covenant. Many churches today use the term *covenant* to speak of God's relationship with Israel and with the Christian community, and of relationships within the Christian community. Preachers with a strong social conscience often refer to the covenant's call for justice in community (especially for the widow, the orphan, the stranger, the poor, the outcast, the exploited, and others denied justice). Preachers in this vein could note how Eurocentric, middle- and upper-class heterosexual males violate covenant in our relations with other individuals and social groups. Middle and upper judicatory leaders like to speak of the covenant between the different expressions of the church—congregations in covenant with middle- and upper-level judicatories. Some Christians believe that the "new covenant" in Jesus Christ has obviated the "old covenant" that God made with Judaism.

Christians tend to speak of the covenant in the singular, as if the biblical tradition contains only one covenant. The preacher could help correct this mistaken viewpoint and could usher the congregation into a conversation on the meaning of covenant by doing a series on different notions of covenant in the Bible. Here is one way of putting together such a series:[2]

1. Covenant with Noah: Genesis 9:1-17.

2. Covenants with Sarah and Abraham: Genesis 15:1-21 (promise of the land); Genesis 17:1-22 (promise of heirs).

3. Covenant at Sinai (Mosaic covenant): Exodus 19:1-8; 20:1-17; excerpts from Exodus 20:22–23:33 (often called the "Book of Covenant").

4. Renewal of the covenant: Joshua 24.

5. Covenant with David: 2 Samuel 7:1-17.

6. Violations of covenant by the community: Jeremiah 11:1-17.

7. A new covenant: Jeremiah 31:31-34.

8. Covenant in the ministry of Jesus: Matthew 26:26-29/Mark 14:22-25.

9. Paul interprets God as faithful to the covenants God made with Israel: Romans 9:1–11:36. Texts for reading in worship: Romans 9:1-5; 11:25-32.

10. Hebrews interprets the covenant through Jesus as superior to the covenants with Israel: Hebrews 8:1-7 (taking into account the context of Hebrews 8:1–9:28).

In this series, in addition to encouraging the congregation to recognize the diversity of covenants in the Torah, Prophets, and Writings, the preacher needs to help the community consider the relationship between covenantal themes in those materials and in the Gospels and Letters. Many preachers, under the impetus of rethinking Christian theology after the Holocaust, argue that Christian supersessionism—the claim that the covenant through Jesus is not only superior to the covenant with Israel but has replaced that covenant—is theologically inappropriate.

A Series on Biblical Characters

A series on biblical characters will be appealing in many congregations because of the fascination with personality today. "Inquiring minds want to know," the popular newspaper slogan has it. We are often curious as to what people are really like, what makes them the way they are, and what happens behind the scenes. The preacher could use this fascination as a point of entry into a series on biblical characters.

At the same time, the minister needs to make clear that the Bible does not partake in the cult of personality in which so many people are absorbed today. Indeed, the Bible seldom reveals matters of psychological interest when it describes characters. When preaching from a biblical character, the preacher should focus not on the personality of the character but on the role the character plays in the document in which the character appears and in the larger stories of Israel and the church. Indeed, ministers need to guard against retrojecting their own psychological and sociological inclinations on the biblical character.

The biblical writers typically present characters for one (or more) of several purposes:

- as vehicles through whom God works

- as figures through whom the biblical writers authorize God's approval or disapproval of particular attitudes, behaviors, and circumstances

- as positive models for human response to God's purposes

- as anti-models of human response to God's purposes (that is, as figures who are unfaithful)

- as ambiguous agents who struggle with how to respond to the divine lure

Frequently the biblical writer wants listeners or readers to identify with a biblical character and to respond accordingly. In the parables, for example, listeners usually identify with the main character and experience the unfolding of the story. If the story contains a surprising turn of events, the listener experiences the surprise.

Almost always, the presence of biblical characters prompts the reader to consider whether we embrace the character (and the attitudes and behaviors represented in the character), turn away from the character's attitudes and behaviors, or do some mixture of both. Many biblical portrayals of characters are intended to cause us to think about how we respond to God's purposes in our own time.

An Example: Women Setting the Pace. While many positions of leadership in the church have become open to women in the last forty years, especially in the long-established Protestant denominations, many congregations and other expressions of the church have reservations about women in such positions. In such a context a preacher might take up a series on women who, in different times and circumstances, set the pace for the communities of their names. They cooperated with God's purposes and carried out faithful leadership. Women today can do the same.

The series that follows, "Women Setting the Pace," identifies women from several different moments in the lives of Israel and the church. When preaching on these figures, the preacher should (per previous statement) honor the place of the character in the documents in which we encounter them.

1. Sarah (Gen. 12:1-3; 18:1-15)
2. Rahab (Josh. 2:1-24)
3. Hannah (1 Sam. 2:1-10)
4. Huldah (2 Kgs. 22:14-20)
5. Ruth (Ruth 1:15-18; 3:6-13)
6. Esther (Esther 7:9-17; 9:20-28)
7. Mary the Mother of Jesus (Luke 1:26-38)
8. Mary and Martha (Luke 10:38-42)
9. Women in leadership in the diaconate and the house churches (Rom. 16:1-16)

Preaching on biblical characters comes with a caution. The Bible does not give enough information about some characters to be the basis of a sermon on that character. Occasionally I see an announcement of a series on the twelve apostles—one sermon on each apostle. But the fact is that the Gospels and Acts simply do not provide enough data on each of the apostles to justify such a complete series. To be sure, a preacher could compare and contrast the lists of names of the apostles, and, more important, how the apostles function in the different Gospels and in Acts (and perhaps in Paul's writings). But the preacher simply does not have enough information about Bartholomew, for instance, to devote a sermon to that character. The same is true of a good many characters in the Bible.

As Many Possibilities for Series from the Bible as Sundays for Preaching

This chapter does not illustrate even a handful of series that a preacher could develop from the Bible. As indicated above, the number of possibilities for series is limited only by the number of Sundays a preacher has available. I close by mentioning some more possibilities for series in abbreviated form. While a preacher might develop some of these series in the congregation, my larger hope is that this list will spark preachers to imagine other series that fit their contexts.

• Pictures of Jesus in the Gospels and Letters. A pastor could develop a series on different understandings of Jesus in Paul's writings, Mark, Matthew, Luke-Acts, Paul's disciples, the Johannine literature, and the book of Revelation.

• Titles for Jesus. What does it mean to call Jesus Son of God, Son of Man, Lord, Son of David, Logos (Word), One Who Reveals God, or High Priest?

• Different genres of biblical literature. A preacher could put together a number of series, each around a different genre of biblical literature. For example: parables, miracle stories, controversy stories, sagas, oracles of judgment, or oracles of salvation. The preacher might select passages that represent a particular type of literature in a particular biblical book, such as miracle stories in Mark or parables in Luke.

• Different kinds of psalms. The book of Psalms contains different kinds of psalms. A series could have one sermon on each of the several types of psalms: individual lament, community lament, individual thanksgiving, community thanksgiving, hymn of praise, royal psalm, enthronement psalm, and others.

• Troubling passages about women. Given the struggles of women across history and into our time, a series highlighting passages on struggles of women in the biblical period might be helpful, for example, Hagar (Gen. 16:1-16; 21:8-21), Dinah (Gen. 24:1-34), Tamar (Gen. 38:1-30), Jephthah's daughter (Judg. 11:1-40), the Levite's concubine (Judg. 19:1-20).

• Wisdom literature. A series could help the congregation encounter the different faces, modes, and concerns of wisdom literature with a sermon each on Job, Proverbs, Ecclesiastes, Song of Songs, and the wisdom psalms. Congregations that acknowledge Wisdom of Solomon and Sirach (Ecclesiasticus) as sacred scripture could include these texts.

• Wisdom personified as a woman. The church is lately recovering a sense of wisdom as a feminine figure. A series could highlight passages that depict Lady Wisdom in operation. Additionally, a preacher might contrast two women: Wisdom and the loose woman, or folly: Proverbs 1:20-33 (contrast with a loose woman: 2:16-19); 3:13-18; 4:5-9; 5:15-19 (contrast with a loose woman: 5:3-14); 7:4-5 (contrast with a prostitute: 7:10-27); 8:3-36, esp.,

22-31; 9:1-6 (contrast with folly: 9:13-18), and possibly Wisdom of Solomon 7:22b–8:16; Sirach (Ecclesiasticus) 24:1-34.

- Notions of what happens at death. A colleague and I recently surveyed our congregations regarding the theological questions uppermost on the minds of the members. To my surprise the biggest single category is, "What happens when we die? What is heaven like?" This soil is ripe for a series on the different notions of what happens to the individual at death: the body disintegrates and the self disappears, but the name lives on in the family; the person goes to Sheol; the person dies and awaits the resurrection; and the essence of the person goes to be with God in heaven at death.

- Prophets in the Deuteronomistic tradition. The Deuteronomists put forward a distinctive (though not entirely unique) view of the prophetic office, beginning with Moses (Deut. 18:9-22), and including Elijah, Elisha, Amos, Hosea, and Jeremiah.

- Barren women giving birth. The barren woman is often a powerful and poignant symbol in the Torah, Prophets, and Writings. While taking care to acknowledge the fullness of the single life and the childless life, a preacher might use God causing birth as a symbol of providence for many who are in barren situations: Genesis 18:1-15; 30:1-24; Judges 13:2-25; 1 Samuel 1:1-28; 2 Kings 4:2-37.

- Single biblical text. Some biblical passages are so meaty that a preacher could work through different perspectives on that one text for three, four, or five weeks.

- Single text: different methods. A preacher could look at the same biblical passage through the lenses of several different methods of interpretation, one a week for several successive weeks. For example: redaction criticism, literary criticism, rhetorical criticism, social science criticism, canonical criticism, performance criticism, ideological criticism, postcolonial criticism, and theological criticism.

CHAPTER 8

Preaching from Doctrines, Practices, and Personal and Social Issues

A physician encounters a symptom in a patient, makes a diagnosis, and prescribes a treatment. Similarly, a preacher sometimes becomes aware of needs in the congregation, reflects on those needs theologically, and points to strategies to address the situation. This chapter focuses on four specific cases of a preacher's diagnostic process: when the preacher becomes aware of the need to speak about Christian doctrine or practices or of the need to provide theological clarity regarding personal or social issues.

The minister hears directly or indirectly the congregation seeking theological guidance or recognizes a need in the community. For example the preacher may hear the congregation ask, "What do we most deeply believe about God?" "How do we pray with confidence?" The preacher may recognize that the congregation needs help sorting out what to do when confronted with certain personal choices or when trying to identify Christian perspectives on a controversial social issue. The preacher then formulates a sermon or a series of sermons to speak to these matters.

This chapter begins with a review of the choices the preacher makes when becoming aware of a need along the lines of doctrine, practice, or a personal or social issue. The heart of the chapter takes up preaching on these matters.

A Preacher's Choices: From the Bible or from the Topic? A Single Sermon or a Series?

When turning to each of the four kinds of needs named in this chapter, the structure of theological analysis is similar. The preacher recognizes the presenting symptom. With the help of resources, the preacher comes to as much theological clarity as possible. Along the way the preacher decides whether to speak to the symptom from the perspective of the Bible or a topical approach. The preacher locates the relationship of the theological interpretation of the presenting symptom to the congregation and develops the sermon accordingly.

Preaching from the Bible

Most ministers typically preach from a biblical text or theme. Indeed, some preachers believe that a message *must* grow from interaction with the Bible in order to qualify as Christian preaching. As the point of departure for the sermon, the preacher must choose a specific biblical text, or group of texts, that helps the preacher address the doctrine, practice, or personal or social issue. In doing so, the preacher needs to respect the otherness of the biblical material and not simply co-opt the Bible for the preacher's own agenda.

A preacher might follow one of three pathways from the Bible to today. First, when a text, or some other configuration of biblical material, speaks immediately to an issue, a minister can bring this material *directly* into the sermon. Second, a preacher may find that while little biblical material relates directly to the focus of the message, a preacher can find an appropriate *analogy* between a situation in the world of the Bible and the situation raising the concern in the congregation. Of course, a pastor needs to handle analogies with respect and precision and not simply project what the pastor would like to find into the analogy. Third, a preacher might also identify a theological trajectory in the biblical material and imagine how that trajectory extends into the contemporary situation.

The Bible may not have the last word on the doctrine, practice, or personal or social issue. Beginning with the biblical text, the sermon could range into the larger reaches of Christian reflection.

Clergy following this path sometimes think they have found a connection between the Bible and the topic where none really exists. When the preacher cannot locate biblical material opening a natural way to address the subject at the center of the sermon, a preacher is advised to take a topical path.

Preaching from a Topical Approach

Another approach holds that the preacher may develop a topical sermon.[1] In the latter case, the preacher interprets a topic—such as a doctrine, a practice, or a personal or social issue—through the lens of the preacher's theology without basing the sermon on a particular biblical text or theme. A topic is an issue that a preacher can better address directly from the perspective of the preacher's deepest theological convictions, rather than going through particular biblical material. In a topical sermon the preacher seeks to help the congregation come to an adequate theological interpretation of the topic at the heart of the sermon. In a sense the preacher's theological conviction or the church's doctrinal or ethical teaching serves as the text of the sermon.

A preacher might turn to a topical sermon when the Bible does not address an issue or when biblical perspectives are hard to access. A preacher might take up a topical approach when an issue is immediately in the face of the congregation and the community is longing for direct theological interpretation. A church's theological interpretation of a topic sometimes transcends the theological perspectives explicitly articulated in the Bible; a topical approach allows for a comprehensive theological point of view. Preachers are sometimes tempted to misuse a biblical text or theme as nothing more than a trampoline to get the sermon subject into the air. A topical trail might be more honest.

To be candid, some topical preaching is theologically vacuous, amounting to little more than warmed-over psychology, sociology, and politics mixed with the minister's biases. But when powered by a critical theological perspective, topical preaching can be an important way of helping congregations come to theological clarity regarding specific issues. Indeed, the topical preacher can sometimes get immediately to the theological heart of an issue without having to deal with exegesis and hermeneutics that are part of working with a biblical text.

A Single Sermon or a Series?

A preacher must decide further whether to preach a single sermon or whether to develop a series of sermons. One sermon may be enough for the size of the subject and its import in the congregation. If the preacher decides to pursue a series, the number of sermons in the series should be enough to cover the subject but within the congregation's attention span.

Preaching on Christian Doctrine

In the broad sense, every sermon should have a theological character and should interact with Christian doctrine and theology.[2] Indeed, on the way to the sermon, the preacher typically moves from a biblical text or theme through the tunnel of Christian doctrine and the preacher's own theology. Additionally, from time to time the congregation needs to focus specifically on core convictions of Christian faith. At times the congregation will raise questions directly. "What do we believe about the virgin birth...about the relationship of wealth and poverty in Christian community...about what happens after death?" At other times the preacher's pastoral listening may reveal that people have questions in the backs of their minds or stirrings in their hearts that they cannot quite articulate. Moreover, pastors can become aware that congregations are malnourished theologically and would benefit from the theological nutrition of sermons that focus on doctrine and theology.

Doctrine

For the purposes of this discussion, I think of doctrine as the church's formal statements of belief as well as the informal assumptions of belief that sometimes function with the near force of doctrine. A few well-known examples of doctrine include:

- Apostolic Affirmation of Faith

- Nicene Affirmation of Faith

- Chalcedonian Formulation

- Augsburg Confession

- Heidelberg Catechism

- Shorter Westminster Catechism

- Thirty Nine Articles of the Anglican and Episcopal Churches

- Baptist Faith and Message

- Statement of Faith of the United Church of Christ

- Confession of Faith of the Evangelical Lutheran Church in America

- A Modern Affirmation of Faith and the Korean Creed of the United Methodist Church

• Book of Discipline of the United Methodist Church

• Statement of Truths of the Assemblies of God

• United Church of Canada Statement of Faith

• Confession of 1967 and A Brief Statement of Faith of the Presbyterian Church (U.S.A.)

• Baltimore Catechism

Churches often generate formal and informal interpretations of their formal doctrinal statements.

Preaching on Doctrine through the Preacher's Theological Lens

To be candid, the preacher often preaches doctrine through the lens of the preacher's own theology.[3] This theology is usually influenced by one or more contemporary theological families, such as liberal theology, mutual critical correlation, process theology, fundamentalism, evangelicalism, neo-orthodoxy, postliberalism, theologies of otherness, liberation theologies, and racial-ethnic theologies.[4] Of course, preachers and theologians within each family formulate the specific content of Christian faith with their own nuances.

Ministers likely preach doctrine through the lens of their particular theological viewpoint.[5] A preacher does not simply preach an assertion such as "I believe in Jesus Christ, [God's] only Son, our Lord...conceived by the power of the Holy Spirit, and born of the virgin Mary" (Apostolic Affirmation of Faith). Preachers interpret this doctrine from the perspective of their theological families. The doctrine of salvation, for instance, might look quite different to a process theologian, a liberation theologian, and a theologian of otherness.

A Series Overviewing Basic Christian Doctrine

Given the collapse of adult education in many congregations and the theological limpidity of a good number of congregations in the historic denominations today, I join many others in thinking that preachers should

131

periodically develop a series overviewing basic Christian doctrine. One honored way to do so is to use a basic affirmation of faith that is important to the congregation and to develop one sermon each week based on one element of that affirmation.

For example, a preacher might use the Apostolic Affirmation of Faith as the framework for a series.

1. I believe in God the Father Almighty, creator of heaven and earth.

2. I believe in Jesus Christ, his only son, our Lord.

3. I believe in the Holy Spirit.

4. I believe in the holy catholic church.

5. I believe in the communion of saints.

6. I believe in the forgiveness of sins.

7. I believe in the resurrection of the body and life everlasting.

Over several years, a preacher could use several different historic and contemporary affirmations as the basis of similar series.

Given the fact that the identity of particular denominations and movements is not now as clear as it used to be, people sometimes wonder, "What does it mean to be a member of the African Methodist Episcopal Church? The Baptist Church? The Church of God in Christ? The Episcopal, United Methodist, or United Presbyterian Churches?" A preacher could profitably create a series around the distinctive beliefs of the denomination or movement.

A Series Exploring Individual Elements of Christian Doctrine

A related approach is to take one element of Christian doctrine and explore its subdivisions. This allows the congregation to come to a more nuanced understanding of the breadth, depth, and complexity of Christian doctrine. The preacher may follow a traditional confession or may subdivide the doctrine. For example, a series on the doctrine of Christ can easily unfold along the elements articulated in the Apostolic Affirmation of Faith.

1. I believe in Jesus Christ, his only Son, our Lord. (This could be used as an introduction to the series by calling attention to the place of Jesus in the history of Israel and in Christian faith.)

2. He was conceived by the Holy Spirit and born of the Virgin Mary.

3. He suffered under Pontius Pilate, was crucified, died, and was buried.

4. He descended to the dead.

5. On the third day he rose again.

6. He ascended into heaven and is seated at the right hand of the Father.

7. He will come again to judge the living and the dead.

The preacher could also shape such a series according to contemporary questions and categories suggested by the preacher's systematic theology or other structures.

Preaching on Christian Practices

In chapter 1 we noted that a strength of the *Revised Common Lectionary* was that the themes of the Christian year become engrained over time in a way analogous to a child learning to play the piano by practice. I have a friend who is a concert-level pianist who regularly plays before thousands of people and who practices every single day except Thanksgiving and Christmas. Over time, he says, he not only learned to play the piano but also became a musician, that is, someone whose whole being is alive to music. Wherever he is and whatever he does, he feels the music of the world, he contributes to the music of the world, and he is part of the music of the world, and it is part of him.

What Is Christian Practice?

In a way similar to the child learning to play the piano and becoming a musician, an important movement in theology points out that practice is essential to the life of the Christian community.[6] At the simplest level, practice is something the church does. My father was a dentist and spoke of his practice, by which he meant both the skills required to be a dentist and the patients he treated. Similarly, we Christians must be able to do essential things by ourselves and with others to be fully (or mostly or partly) Christian.

At the same time, Christian identity is more than a skill set. It is more than being able to do certain things. Christian identity is who we are. It is a way of being that permeates the mind, heart, and will. We learn how to engage in Christian practice by practicing, that is, by doing the things that are central to Christian identity over and over, which matures us as Christians. Practice thus both *forms* the church and is a means through which the church *expresses* its identity. We become what we practice.

E. Byron Anderson, who teaches at Garrett Evangelical Theological School, speaks of worship as "practicing ourselves."[7] The notion of practicing here is a multiple entendre: through worship we practice, or rehearse, how we are to live the rest of the week. This type of practice leads to a second type of practice—putting what we rehearsed in the sanctuary into effect in everyday life. Preaching and listening to sermons are themselves part of the practice of worship.

When preaching on a practice, the preacher needs to clarify the nature and purpose of the practice.

- What does the congregation need to know about the practice?

- How is the practice intended to help the congregation strengthen its identity, its life as Christian community, and its witness in the larger world?

- How does the congregation put the practice into practice in its life and beyond?

A Series on Foundational Christian Practices

A preacher might do a series on several foundational Christian practices. Each week the sermon would focus on a particular practice. For example:

1. Baptism

2. Worship

3. Bible study

4. Prayer

5. Hospitality

6. Working with others for justice

A Series on a Christian Practice

A preacher might also do a series on a particular Christian practice. The sermon each week would focus on a different emphasis within the Christian practice. For example, a series of sermons might focus on how the parts of worship help Christians practice the ways they live throughout the week. What we do liturgically in the various parts of the service is practice for living those same things in the world beyond the sanctuary.

1. Call to worship: gathers the community for worship, thereby reminding us that Christian identity is communal and that our purpose in life is to respond to God's grace and call.

2. Confession of sin and assurance of pardon: naming and taking responsibility for ways in which we violate God's purposes and receiving pardon, which reminds us that God has forgiven us so that we are no longer controlled by the violations of the past but can participate with God in moving toward a more faithful future.

3. Passing the peace: blessing one another with the reminder that God wills for all to live in peace and using the occasion to reconcile (create a relationship of peace) with those with whom we are in conflict.

4. Hearing the reading of the Bible and listening to the sermon: discerning how to recognize God's presence and purposes in the congregation and in the world, and how to respond appropriately.[8]

5. Receiving the loaf and the cup: experiencing God's empowering presence through the loaf and the cup to help us recognize that presence outside the sanctuary

6. Offering: we offer ourselves for God's use throughout the week

Some Other Christian Practices

Given the diversity of Christian communities, each with its distinctive life, the number of practices in the wider Christian family is mind-boggling. The following examples are drawn from some influential discussions of Christian practice:[9]

Honoring the body
Hospitality

135

Household economics
Saying yes and saying no
Keeping Sabbath
Giving testimony
Discernment
Forgiveness
Healing
Dying well
Singing our lives
Learning
Teaching
Telling the truth to one another in love
Naming and protesting injustice
Criticizing and resisting the principalities and the powers
Suffering with one another
Carrying out acts of service

Preaching from Personal and Social Issues

While it may seem strange to speak of personal and social issues together, the pattern of theologically analyzing a personal issue is sufficiently similar to the pattern of theologically analyzing a social issue that we can discuss them at the same time. Indeed, the categories of personal issue and social issue are often integrally related.[10]

Identity in Community in Recent Thinking about the Church

In recent years, many Christian leaders have rediscovered the communal nature of Christian identity. Christian life is not simply a matter of isolated individuals coming to faith. The church is not just a collection of individuals. The church, like Israel, is a community in which individuals are inherently related with one another, as when Paul describes the church as the "body of Christ" (for example, 1 Cor. 12:1–14:40).

From this perspective, the church as community is always present in the individual. The individual always represents the body of Christ. Postmodern thinkers encourage us to recover a sense of the communal. Sermons rightly blast away at the rabid individualism assumed by many people of European origin in North America, and call listeners to recognize the inherent interconnectedness of all in the congregation and, indeed, all human families and creation itself.

Interrelatedness in Personal and Social Issues

Because of this permeating emphasis on community in recent ecclesial conversation, some readers may think a section on *personal* issues is a mistake, especially alongside *social* issues. I can imagine the reader soaked with communal consciousness asking, "But aren't *all* issues social?" Indeed, all personal issues take place in communal contexts, and all personal decisions and actions have social effects. Moreover, all personal decisions are affected by systems that create certain possibilities and take away others.

What I have in mind by personal issues and social issues is not a bald dichotomy, but recognition that even though individuals live in overlapping social networks, some issues come to us in immediately personal ways while others come to us from larger social contexts.

The distinctions between personal and social issues are often mainly matters of focus. The two dimensions are often related in particular cases such that the preacher may not be able to distinguish between the personal and the social but must deal with the issue in both dimensions.

Encountering and Preaching on Personal Issues

We experience some issues personally (even as we experience them in connection with other people) and make decisions about them as individuals or couples or friends or households. *I* must make certain decisions even as I do so as a member of *a larger body*. The community cannot make certain decisions for me even as it provides support, raises questions, and calls me to consider the implications of particular personal decisions. Individuals have considerable agency in connection with these issues. What we think and do has an immediate effect. For example, what should I think about divorce and how should I act in relationship with my good friend who is going through divorce? My relative or partner for whom I have legal responsibility has a terminal illness. Should I request that extreme measures not be taken to lengthen this person's life?

Personal issues come to the preacher's attention in as many ways as there are people. Members of the congregation sometimes literally come to the preacher with personal issues. People visit the office or invite the pastor to the home or stop the preacher in the aisle at the grocery store to talk about an issue. Preachers sometimes become aware of personal issues by paying attention to things that happen in ongoing pastoral life, e.g. the questions people raise, the fears they voice, and the uncertainties with which they wrestle.

137

A preacher could preach one sermon focused on a particular personal issue or could put together a series that deals with several personal issues, each sermon focusing on one. Examples of such personal issues include:

Abortion
Dealing with anger
Divorce
Drug use
End-of-life decisions
Greed
Marriage
Moving from one community to another
Terminal illness
Unemployment
Sex outside of marriage

A preacher could also develop a series of sermons exploring different aspects of one personal issue. Here is a sample sermon series on God's purposes for sex.

1. Introduction to God's purposes for sex

2. God's purposes for sex in a heterosexual relationship

3. God's purposes for sex in the single life

4. God's purposes for sex in a same-sex relationship

5. God's purposes when sexual infidelity occurs

Encountering and Preaching on Social Issues

Social issues arise from social circumstances in the larger social world, and typically involve social forces and systems. While social issues may originate or be manifest in circumstances far away, they often have consequences for people in the congregation. War and racism may be systemic in character, but people personally feel their effects. A child serving in the military is killed. People of color are overlooked as if they do not exist.

We often respond to social issues with questions, opinions, emotions, and desires, but feel that our agency is limited. Whether true or not, we sometimes feel that our individual actions will have little immediate effect. Preachers may need to help the congregation name what they *can* do in the way of Christian witness even if the witness does not promise an immediate and ultimate fix.

Social issues become a part of the purview of preacher and congregation in multiple ways. Issues burst into the media. People may ask the preacher for a Christian interpretation of an issue, or the preacher may notice otherwise that the congregation would like a better theological grip on a social issue. The pulpit may be ripe for a consideration of social issues that came to the preacher's attention during the course of pastoral life. A preacher hears and sees things that point to the need for a sermon on a social issue, even if the congregation has not reached such a point of awareness.

A recent commentary on the lectionary from the perspective of social justice offers a list of eighty-four representative social issues on which a preacher could focus a sermon or series of sermons.[11] A random sample of topics reveals their breadth:

Affirmative action
Anti-Semitism
Drug cartels
Environmental crisis
Flight to the suburbs
Genocide
Health care
Human rights
Immigration
Police brutality
Racism
Reproductive rights
Terrorism
Xenophobia

A preacher could also develop a series of sermons on one social issue. Here is a sample sermon series on racism in a congregation of European origin.

1. What is racism? Naming racism in the congregation and the larger social world

2. Effects of racism on people of color

3. Effects of racism on Eurocentric people

4. Becoming an anti-racist/pro-reconciling church

5. Working toward an anti-racist/reconciling world

A Path to Preaching Theologically about Personal and Social Issues

A path to preparing the sermon on personal and social issues often includes the following.

Naming the Issue

The preacher may need to help the congregation name an issue in theological terms. The congregation may be unaware of issues to which they need to give theological or ethical consideration. In such cases, the preacher may help the congregation realize the presence and effects of social issues and the importance of coming to a theological interpretation.

Helping the Congregation See Connections between the Personal and the Social

Many issues have immediate personal effects but social causes. The personal effects may be so powerful that they obscure the connection to larger social roots. For optimum Christian response, the preacher may need to encourage the congregation to recognize not only God's presence in the personal distress caused by the issue but also the importance of addressing the larger matter.

For example, a number of people may lose their jobs when a local factory closes. They have the immediate personal experience of being unemployed. They need support in the immediate moment. The congregation may also need to see that the closing of the factory is part of a larger transnational economic system that benefits a relatively small number of stockholders.

A sense of pastoral timing may come into play. The closing of the factory may create such a shock that people are unable to consider the larger issues. The preacher may need to delay bringing systemic questions into the conversation until people are better able to think about the bigger picture.

Help People Recognize What They Can Do

A preacher may need to help the congregation recognize the difference between coping and becoming agents in transformation. When the effects of an issue erupt into consciousness and people are raw, the work of the pastor may first be to help the congregation cope with the situation. At a better time the preacher might help the community consider the possibility of becoming an agent of transformation in relationship to that issue.

Avoiding the Amateur Syndrome

When I was once a guest Bible teacher in congregation, a local member recollected an earlier minister in that congregation whose sermons were rife with self-help psychology. This person thought those sermons were more like group therapy than preaching, "And that preacher did not have any training in group therapy." The conclusion: "There is nothing so amateurish as a preacher who has read an article on the Internet and stands up in the pulpit and talks like an expert."

This local sage reminds us that preachers need to be adequately informed about the subject of the sermon. This may involve research. If so, preachers want to do their homework so they do not fall victim to the amateur syndrome in which they have just enough knowledge to reveal what they do not know.

Goals of Preaching on Personal and Social Issues

One general goal of preaching on personal and social issues is to help the congregation move toward a theological interpretation of the issue and appropriate responses. A correlate goal of preaching on personal issues is to strengthen individuals so they can be more effective members of the social world. Preaching on social issues aims to help the social world become the kind of arena that nurtures individuals in ways that optimize their contributions to community. In this complicated network of relationships, one thing is for sure: God is present at every moment in preparation and embodiment, and afterwards. God offers support, challenge, and invitation as appropriate to each occasion.

CHAPTER 9

Preaching from a Free Selection of Biblical Texts or Themes

While working on this chapter, I was having lunch with clergy friends when one asked, "What are you writing now?" After hearing about the chapter, a table companion who preaches from the lectionary said, "Can you give me a discount on the book equal to the cost of that chapter? I will never read that chapter because I never choose my own text." Suddenly inspired, another minister burst out, "Well, then, can you give me a discount equal to the rest of the book since I will only read the chapter on choosing your text? That is the only way I preach."

Through further conversation, we discovered that neither one is quite right. The preacher from the lectionary tradition does make a choice every week. "Do I preach from the Gospel, the Epistle, the third reading (from the Torah, Prophets, and Writings), or the psalm? Do I bring more than one text into the sermon?" Moreover, this preacher sometimes brings the homily in situations in which she does choose a text—at a church retreat, the community-wide Martin Luther King Jr. Day Service, and weddings and funerals. The preacher from the free-selection tradition was preparing a sermon for an upcoming Week of Christian Unity, whose text was assigned by the national planners of the Week.

This chapter begins with a drive down the open road of freely selecting the text, the hazards that can beset this practice, and what a preacher should consider when working with a freely selected text. The chapter concludes with a probe of one-shot preaching assignments—occasions when the preacher is in a pulpit for only one sermon.[1]

Open Road When Freely Selecting Texts

A lectionary is a limited access road. By contrast, free selection is an open access highway to the sermon. The preacher can travel at the preacher's own speed on a route of the preacher's own choosing, taking side roads, stopping along the way, following detours, and shooting down unexplored roads. We look now at characteristics of this direction before turning to potential road hazards.

Bringing Together Text and Context

One of the preacher's primary purposes is to help the congregation interpret God's presence and leading in the context in which the congregation lives and consider how to respond appropriately. The biblical text offers an understanding of the divine leading and of appropriate responses to that leading. In the sermon, the preacher engages in a conversation with the text and the congregation, exploring how interaction with the text helps the congregation come to as clear and confident an interpretation as possible. A text can facilitate or complicate this conversation.

While preachers working from the lectionary often comment on how often the text fits the situation, the fact is that the lectionary text and the situation of the congregation are sometimes distant.

The great strength of freely selecting a text is the preacher's ability to identify a passage from the Bible that fits the context of the moment of preaching. The preacher looks for a text with a theological trajectory that correlates with the immediate world of the congregation. The conversation can then honor the otherness of the text while moving directly and deeply to the concerns on the mind and heart of the congregation.

The Entire Bible Is Available to the Preacher—Every Single Verse

Free selection makes the entire Bible, every single verse, available to the preacher. While the *Revised Common Lectionary* brings a lot of the Bible into the purview of the congregation, it omits many passages and even some entire books. The congregation that follows the lectionary in perpetuity is thus denied access to those materials. While the lectionary brings some passages onto the preacher's screen that the preacher might otherwise avoid, the lectionary also prevents the preacher from encountering certain passages. By contrast, free selection opens the whole Bible.

The Preacher Can Immediately Bring Appropriate Biblical Material to Fresh Circumstances

Congregations occasionally face dramatic changes in circumstance. A natural disaster sweeps through town. A beloved member of the congregation is in an automobile accident on Saturday and hangs between life and death when the congregation gathers for worship. A world event, a national event, an event in the municipality—something happens to galvanize the congregation's attention. Pastors who determine their own texts and who have the Bible in their bones (see page 148) can quickly locate passages that correlate with their situations.

Preachers Can Follow Their Passions in the Bible

Preachers often have a passion for particular biblical materials. A preacher's passion is often enough to stir congregational interest as when a listener thinks, "I want to know why our minister is so drawn to this material." Free choice of the text allows preachers to pursue their passions in biblical literature in immediate ways that are sometimes blocked by other methods of selection

To be sure, preachers do not want to flood the congregation with too much of their passion in too short a time with too little critical reflection. The result of such an approach can be similar to a rainstorm dumping more water on a low-lying street than storm sewers can handle. In communities in which the storm sewers and the conventional sewers are connected, a hard rain can bring sewage into the street. But when preachers draw the energy from their passions, the result can be a magnetic sermon.

Hazards When Freely Selecting Texts

These road hazards will not be in every preacher's pathway when freely selecting biblical texts. But preachers can adjust their homiletical driving patterns when these hazards occur in the driving lane.

Turning Again and Again to the Same Biblical Material

One of the greatest hazards in free selection is the possibility of the preacher returning again and again to the same biblical material. This can be boring to both preacher and congregation. The preacher can assume a familiarity that anesthetizes the preacher to the otherness of the biblical material. Perhaps worst of all, focusing on too small a sphere of biblical material can limit the contact of the preacher and the congregation with the "depth of the riches and wisdom and knowledge of God" (Rom. 11:33) in the Bible. Indeed, preaching from the same places in scripture time after time can actually give the congregation a warped view of God's purposes and of Christian life and witness by leaving the impression that the view of that slice of biblical material is *the* view of the whole Bible.

In their own way, lectionary preachers sometimes fall victim to this hazard. Many lectionary preachers turn again and again to the Gospel text without serious thinking about the preaching potentials of the Epistle; the reading from the Torah, Prophets, and Writings; or the psalm. While this may not be as confining as resorting to the same text or texts, it is still limiting.

Preachers Can Easily Interpret a Text as a Mirror of Their Preconceived Agendas

Every preacher faces a major theological temptation: to read the preacher's own theology and theological, ecclesial, and social agendas into the text. When ministers begin to choose a text, they sometimes think they already know what they want to say, so they look for a text to confirm their viewpoint without really taking into account whether a text moves in that direction. In such moments, preachers *use* the text for their own purposes. The preacher does not respect the otherness of the text but instead reads the text as an extension of the preacher's own perceptions. In this way, the pastor can violate the integrity of the text.

This hazard is in the preacher's roadway whether the preacher begins sermon preparation in concert with a lectionary, with preaching continuously, or when developing a series, but it is most potent when freely picking one's own text. The danger is compounded if the preacher returns again and again to the same covey of texts because the preacher can so easily think, "I've been here before." The immediate presence of an array of texts, as in the lectionary, can remind the preacher that the biblical writers have their own theologies and thus prompt the preacher to respect the otherness of the text.

Preachers Can Feel Desperate and Make Poor Choices

Preachers who choose their own texts from week to week can live so much hand to mouth that they may make poor choices of texts. By way of embarrassing confession, when I operated under the rubric of free selection while serving congregations, I sometimes let the rising water of ministerial responsibilities overwhelm much of the time I should have given to sermon preparation. I also spent too much time simply *choosing* the text. "Well, this one looks good...and so does that one...but what about the one back here...?" Sunday drew near. A feeling of desperation gripped my insides. I grabbed the next text that floated down the stream of consciousness.

From Week to Week, Sermons Can Bounce Like Pinballs

In the bygone electronic world of the 1960s, 1970s, and 1980s, arcades often contained pinball machines. In the heat of the game, a hard ball bounced around a large, flat game board containing posts, side mounts, and other fixtures to push the ball so it careened from one fixture to another. When clergy select their own texts, sermons over several weeks sometimes bounce from one passage to another, from one historical situation to another, from one social agenda to another, or from one theological view to another in the same way the ball careens inside the pinball machine. If this pattern becomes a way of life, the congregation may feel bruised by bouncing from place to place.

When Working with a Freely Selected Text

When choosing their own texts, pastors can do simple things to help sermons develop in full-bodied ways. There are no surprises here, but in a world in which it is so easy to be sidetracked, basic reminders sometimes function as traffic cones marking reliable lanes.

Honor the Fullness of the Text in Its Historical, Literary, and Theological Contexts

Preachers sometimes select a text because the preacher thinks one part of it speaks to the context of the congregation—a word, an image, a phrase. Sometimes the text comes to mind not because of something in the text itself but because of the preacher's association with the text. In such circumstances a preacher can easily use the text as a springboard to what the preacher wants to say without respecting the otherness of the text.

Every preacher in *every* situation of working with a passage of the Bible should honor the historical, literary, and theological contexts of the passage. If the preacher engages the text in a responsible exegetical fashion and discovers that the text does not support the preacher's agenda, then the preacher must look for another text. If the preacher's purpose is theologically appropriate but is not connected to particular biblical texts, the preacher might consider a topical sermon (see chapter 8).

The Bible in Their Bones

Preachers who freely choose their own passages need to have the Bible in their bones. Indeed, these preachers need to have thoroughgoing familiarity with both the content of the Bible and with the critical interpretation of the Bible. The preacher needs to know what is within the pages of the sacred book and what to do when opening its pages.

If ministers are aware of only certain parts of the Bible, or if their knowledge of the Bible as a whole is only cursory, then their resources for making a critically informed choice of text are limited. Ministers with a minimal working canon can easily overlook biblical materials that are pertinent to their context but are not in their canon. Such ministers have a propensity to turn to those parts of the Bible with which they are familiar. The congregation is thus denied access to biblical materials that could be significant conversation partners.

Do Not Choose to Please or Punish

A preacher needs to choose a text whose voice has the potential to help both preacher and people ponder God's presence and leading. When choosing texts during my own weekly preaching days, I had unfortunate tendencies that may be present in other preachers. I would sometimes choose texts that would please the congregation or that were easy passages with which to work. Such choices avoided conflict with the congregation and made preparation easier. I sometimes avoided texts that would be difficult in our context because they were hard to explain, or because they reinforced theological, ethical, or political tendencies in the congregation that I wanted to suppress, or because they raised issues that could cause conflict in the congregation. When I was disappointed with the congregation, I would sometimes choose texts that would have a punitive effect on the church. Through the text, I could scold the congregation or project some of my own hostility onto the congregation. Such motives are not worthy.

A preacher needs to employ critical self-awareness when freely identifying passages as the starting point for the sermon. Under the watchful eye of critical reflection, a preacher may rightly choose a text because it reinforces tendencies in the congregation that should be amplified. A pastor may turn to a particular text because of its prophetic potential for helping the congregation recognize and redress points at which they need to live and witness more faithfully.

Congregation Might Help Select the Text

While preachers usually choose the text on the basis of their own pastoral listening, preachers might also solicit suggestions from the congregation. A clergy couple I know periodically invites their congregation to indicate Bible passages and other topics on which they would like to hear sermons. Insofar as is possible and appropriate, this longtime clergy couple develops sermons on these texts. The ministers often visit the people who nominated texts to ascertain where the interest in the text originated and the particular questions the parishioners bring to the text and its place in larger Christian theology. These ministers report that the congregation is noticeably attentive during these messages and that attendance often goes up when the sermon touches on a text or topic of special interest to the congregation.

Courage When Preaching from Difficult Texts

From time to time, preachers need to think with the congregation about difficult matters within the congregation or in the congregation's complicity with injustice beyond the church walls. It takes courage for any preacher to move in such directions. A lectionary preacher gets a little help in introducing such subjects when there is a natural bridge from the assigned lectionary readings to the situation. "Our text for today brings me to think about a tender but important matter."

Preachers who select texts may need to stand on their own feet before the congregation to explain why they have turned to the particular text and subject matter. These preachers have support for turning to the text because it is in the Bible, but they do not have the support of the wider church represented by finding a text in the lectionary. I do not know that a freely selecting preacher needs any more courage than a lectionary preacher, but I am confident that freely selecting preachers must have a full measure of courage to take up difficult material.

Help Yourself and the Worship Leaders by Planning Ahead

Ministers who freely select passages for preaching can help themselves and other worship leaders by planning in advance. Preachers can select texts as well as identify preliminary issues and questions to address in exegesis, theological reflection, and hermeneutic. A preacher might list possible directions for future sermons. Of course, impulses in planning (no matter how great the spark) need to be checked against disciplined exegesis and reflection. Working in this fashion, a preacher could plan a month, a quarter, six months, or a year in advance. While some preachers can plan effectively in the office, others find it useful to work in atmospheres with less distraction, such as the local coffee shop, the patio at home, or a retreat in a mountain cabin.

A text chosen in July at a cabin beside a fresh flowing mountain spring can sound quite different in late November when the chief operating officer of a large company in town has just announced a plant will close, thus making 20 percent of the congregation unemployed. In such circumstances, the preacher can always make a change of text. Many preachers find it easier to make changes in plans for preaching than to grasp from week to week in search of fresh starting points for the sermon.

Conduct a Regular Inventory of Preaching Texts

To put this concern positively, preachers who name their own texts should regularly conduct an inventory of their preaching to see that, over time, they help the congregation encounter significant parts of the Bible. They also want to help the people consider formative theological issues, take account of important concerns in the congregation, and look at the larger world through a comprehensive theological and ethical lens.

To put this concern negatively, preachers who name their own texts should regularly conduct an inventory of their preaching to see that they are not mired in limited parts of the Bible, or preaching through a narrow theological prism, or beating the same ecclesial issues over and over, or looking at the larger world in warped ways. We can fall into ruts that become the extent of the homiletical pathways we hike.

While it is especially important for clergy who choose their own texts to inventory the emphases in their sermons, clergy should do the same when preaching from the lectionary, from continuous selection, and from series. While such preachers might be less inclined to focus on limited parts of the Bible, they can still fall into patterns that limit the congregation's exposure to theological themes, ecclesial considerations, and ethical issues that are optimum for the congregation's growth.

The One-Shot Preaching Assignment

This chapter ends with a brief look at occasions when preachers have the opportunity (or obligation) to select their own texts: the one-shot preaching assignment, that is, occasions when the pastor will preach just one sermon to a particular gathering.[2] One-shot preaching assignments include events such as a congregational retreat held at a church camp, a revival meeting in another congregation, a pulpit exchange, preaching for a middle or upper judicatory gathering, a baccalaureate service, a service in a senior citizen facility, a service in a jail or prison, a service in a hospital chapel, vespers on a local radio or television station, and community-wide services on particular days such as Martin Luther King Jr. Day, Good Friday, Holocaust Memorial Day, Memorial Day, Fourth of July, or Thanksgiving Day. Weddings and funerals sometimes lean toward this category when they take place in unusual settings or involve a large percentage of people who are not members of the congregation.

The preacher should calibrate the purpose of preaching to the specific dynamics of the event. The preacher is called to help the community interpret some aspect of the primary concern of the occasion from the perspective of God's presence and purposes. On Martin Luther King Jr. Day, for instance, preachers might explore how God seeks to create beloved community among the various racial and ethnic groups in the city.

Things to Take into Account

A preacher's temptation may be to go to the barrel for a sermon for the one-shot preaching assignment. However, preparing a fresh sermon usually better honors God, the purposes of preaching, the listeners, and the preacher's own sense of faithfulness and integrity. Insofar as possible, a preacher needs to take into account a number of dynamics pertaining to the one-shot preaching assignment.

- Be clear about the overall purpose of the event and the particular place of the sermon in the event. Evaluate the degree to which the purpose is consistent with your theology, and figure out an appropriate theological relationship with the event. If there is a serious difference between your theology and that of the people at the event, consider how to negotiate the difference.

- Find out as much as you can about the social locations of the people who will be present: ages, sex and sexual orientations, racial and ethnic identities, religious affiliations and theological and ethical viewpoints, the economic situation of the area, the social classes in the congregation, political inclinations, and the relationships (or non-relationships) of the participants to one another.

• Try to identify the most important assumptions, values, symbols, customs, and practices of the group with whom you are speaking. How do these qualities compare and contrast with your own theological values?

• Talk with local ministers or other leaders who can help you get a feel for local culture, especially questions and issues on people's minds, tensions in the community, and other concerns that might not be obvious to you as an outsider but that are important to locals. You want way to get the lay of the land to avoid innocently stepping on land mines in the sermon that would destroy the listening ethos.

• Select a preaching text that has the power to spark a conversation with the congregation that will serve the purposes of the event and of the sermon.

• Ask to read your own scripture lesson, preferably immediately prior to preaching. This gives the congregation a chance to adjust to your voice, and it gives you the chance to inflect the oral performance of the passage with meanings that will serve the sermon.

• At the event itself, before reading the biblical passage from which you will preach, you might call attention to personal relationships you have with the event or with folk who are present. This can help create a sense of community between the congregation and you. In many settings, what you say is empowered by who you know. If the congregation believes you are one of them, they are likely to pay attention to what you have to say.

• In the sermon, use material from your aforementioned research with which the congregation can identify. You can likely find ways to refer to things in the world of the participants. Humor can be especially effective here. On the other hand, you do not want to portray yourself as having firsthand knowledge when you do not. You can phrase your discoveries in ways that respect the secondhand status of your information. "I have heard...Someone told me...On the way through town, I noticed..."

152

- Clarify how long you are to preach. If you are part of a long event with multiple parts, such as a day long ecclesial assembly, plan to preach 20 to 40 percent less than your allotted time in case the event gets behind schedule. You have a responsibility to the event to help it achieve its overall goal. If the planners say you have thirty minutes, but you stand up to preach fifteen minutes after you are scheduled to begin, some attendees will be distracted by the time element. You will have a better chance of communicating with them if you can move briskly through the sermon.

- If you are to bring greetings to the assembly from your institution, try to phrase the greetings in a manner that has a personal tie to the people at the event. Some greetings are set out in such an abstract way that the congregation knows they are not sincere. Some greetings are so pompous that I get the impression their real purpose is to impress the congregation with the self-importance of the speaker and her or his institution.

- Communicate in a timely manner with the planning committee when they want a title, scripture lesson, biographical sketch, and picture.

- Be prepared for a let down when you get home. At some events, you will be a center of attention and treated as a recognized authority whose every word is noted. Indeed, you will sometimes be treated like a god or goddess. But when you get back to your own congregation, you are Linda or Ron, who still has to write an article for the website, recruit a youth group sponsor, find someone to fix the carpet on the stairs, call in the hospital, and prepare a Bible study for the six octogenarians who will be at the church on Wednesday morning. Going home can remind one of the humility that should be at the core of the genuine Christian life. "I am not here to be served (by the attention I received at the one-shot event) but to serve the purposes of God in the everyday community to which I am called."

Preachers are sometimes tempted to dismiss the importance of the one-shot speaking assignment. "I can't even remember who preached my baccalaureate, much less what they said." However, people often remember sermons they heard at a special life moment when faced with questions, decisions, issues, and tensions. One-shot sermons often take place at such crossing points. You never know who might be open to transformation when you stand up to preach. Such opportunities deserve your best attention.

NOTES

Introduction

1. The Christian year is sometimes known as *the church year* or *the liturgical year*. Although churches have had multiple lectionaries over the years, the *Revised Common Lectionary* seems to be the most widely used today. The abbreviation RCL in this book refers to that lectionary. See The Consultation on Common Texts, *The Revised Common Lectionary* (Nashville: Abingdon Press, 1992).

2. The most widely accepted foundational document of the ecumenical expression of this approach is *Baptism, Eucharist, and Ministry* (Geneva: World Council of Churches, 1982).

3. Toward this end, the Bishops' Committee on Priestly Life and Ministry of the United States Conference of Catholic Bishops developed a pivotal document: *Fulfilled in Your Hearing: The Homily in the Sunday Assembly* (Washington, DC: United States Conference of Catholic Bishops, 1982).

4. The Consultation on Common Texts, *Common Lectionary* (New York: Church Hymnal Corporation, 1983).

5. The Consultation on Common Texts, *The Revised Common Lectionary* (Nashville: Abingdon Press, 1992).

6. David G. Buttrick, "Preaching the Lectionary: Two Cheers and Some Questions," *Call to Worship* 37, no. 1 (2002–2003): 52–60.

7. Ronald J. Allen and Clark M. Williamson, *Preaching the Gospels without Blaming the Jews: A Lectionary Commentary; Preaching the Letters without Dismissing the Law: A Lectionary Commentary;* and *Preaching the Old Testament: A Lectionary Commentary* (Louisville: Westminster John Knox Press, 2004, 2006, 2007).

8. Ronald J. Allen, Dale P. Andrews, and Dawn Ottoni-Wilhelm, *Preaching God's Transforming Justice: A Lectionary Commentary, Year B, Featuring 22 New Holy Days for Justice* (Louisville: Westminster John Knox Press, 2011); Dale P. Andrews, Dawn Ottoni-Wilhelm, and Ronald J. Allen, *Preaching God's Transforming Justice: A Lectionary Commentary, Year C, Featuring 22 New Holy Days for Justice* (Louisville: Westminster John Knox Press, 2012); Dawn Ottoni-Wilhelm, Dale P. Andrews, and Ronald J. Allen, *Preaching God's Transforming Justice: A Lectionary*

Commentary, Year A, Featuring 22 New Holy Days for Justice (Louisville: Westminster John Knox Press, 2013).

9. Keith Watkins, Ronald J. Allen, Michael K. Kinnamon, Linda McKiernan-Allen, Katherine N. Kinnamon, *Thankful Praise: A Resource for Christian Worship* (St. Louis: CBP Press, 1987).

10. O. Wesley Allen Jr., *The Homiletic of All Believers: A Conversational Approach* (Louisville: Westminster John Knox Press, 2005), 58–85; idem., *Preaching and Reading the Lectionary: A Three-Dimensional Approach to the Liturgical Year* (St. Louis: Chalice Press, 2007).

11. For easy-to-read introductions to social location, see Ronald J. Allen, *Preaching and the Other: Studies of Postmodern Insights* (St. Louis: Chalice Press, 2009), 5–94; and Ronald D. Sisk, *Preaching Ethically: Being True to the Gospel, Your Congregation and Yourself* (Herndon, VA: Alban Institute, 2008): 1–12.

12. See Ronald J. Allen, *Interpreting the Gospel: An Introduction to Preaching* (St. Louis: Chalice Press, 1998), 63–96; idem, "Preaching as Mutual Critical Correlation," in Jana Childers, ed., *Purposes of Preaching* (St. Louis: Chalice Press, 2004), 1–22. For a similar but more developed approach, see O. Wesley Allen, Jr., *The Homiletic of All Believers: A Conversational Approach to Proclamation and Preaching* (Louisville: Westminster John Knox, 2005). I am also influenced by John S. McClure, *Other-wise Preaching: A Postmodern Ethic for Homiletics* (St. Louis: Chalice Press, 2001) and Lucy Atkinson Rose, *Sharing the Word: Preaching in the Round Table Church* (Louisville: Westminster John Knox Press, 1997).

13. Ronald J. Allen, "Torah, Prophets, Writings, Gospels, Letters: A New Name for the Old Book," *Encounter* 68 (2007): 53–62.

1. Preaching from the Christian Year

1. Adolf Adam, *The Liturgical Year: Its History and Its Meaning after the Reform of the Liturgy* (New York: Pueblo, 1981), offers a traditional scholarly consensus on the origins of the Christian year. Thomas Talley, *The Origins of the Liturgical Year*, 2nd ed. (New York: Pueblo, 1991), offers revised views. A recent discussion in the spirit of Talley is Paul F. Bradshaw and Maxwell E. Johnson, *The Origins of Feasts and Seasons in Early Christianity* (Collegeville: Liturgical Press, 2011).

2. Scholars often use the word *deuteronomic* to refer to material found in the book of Deuteronomy, especially chapters 5–28, and the word *Deuteronomistic* to refer to the point of view of the deuteronomic theology that shapes the present forms of Deuteronomy, Joshua, Judges, the Samuels, the Kings, and some other writings.

3. The Johannine writings are based less on the notion that history is divided into two ages and more on the notion that existence is divided into two spheres: the heavenly sphere of light, truth, sight, freedom, abundance, and life, where God dwells; and the worldly sphere of darkness, lying, blindness, slavery, scarcity, and death, where human beings dwell. For John, God sent Jesus to reveal the possibility of living as a colony of heaven in the midst of the world. The resurrection is the definitive revelation of the truth of that promise. On these different worldviews,

see Ronald J. Allen, *The Life of Jesus for Today,* For Today Series (Louisville: Westminster John Knox Press, 2008), 19–27, 82–90.

4. Language related to Jesus' coming again is commonplace in Christian community past and present. Many Christians believe in a physical apocalypse: God ending the present world and replacing it with a new cosmos. Because the language and ideas of the second coming are so prominent in Christian tradition, I use them in this book. In the interest of theological integrity, however, I indicate that I do not anticipate such a singular cosmic event. As a process (relational) theologian, I believe that God is ever and always present, attempting to lure humankind and nature toward God's purposes of love, peace, justice, community, and abundance. For contemporary theological and hermeneutical purposes, I take the traditional language associated with the second coming to mean that God is not satisfied with life as it is and continually offers possibilities for renewal.

5. For an example of suggestions for preaching from the themes of the Christian year apart from a lectionary, see David Steel, *Preaching Through the Year* (Atlanta: John Knox Press, 1980).

6. Although the *Revised Common Lectionary* brings Johannine texts into the readings, these texts effectively serve end-time theology. On differences between end-time and Johannine theology, see p. 156, n. 3.

7. Among the many accessible guides to the Christian year: Frank C. Senn, *Introduction to Christian Liturgy* (Minneapolis: Fortress Press, 2012), 97–154; Robert E. Webber, *Ancient-Future Worship: Proclaiming and Enacting God's Narrative* (Grand Rapids: Baker Book Co., 2008); Martin Connell, *An Introduction to the Church's Liturgical Year* (Chicago: Loyola Press, 1997).

8. One of the best guides to the Christian year is Laurence Hull Stookey, *Calendar: Christ's Time for the Church* (Nashville: Abingdon Press, 1996). A more comprehensive work is Martin Connell, *Eternity Today, On the Liturgical Year: On God and Time, Advent, Christmas, Epiphany, Candlemas* (New York: Continuum, 2006) vol. 1; idem. *Eternity Today, On the Liturgical Year: Sunday, Lent, The Three Days, The Easter Season, Ordinary Time* (New York: Continuum, 2006), vol. 2. There are many popular introductions to the Christian year, for example, Kimberly Conway Ireton, *The Circle of the Seasons: Meeting God in the Church Year* (Downers Grove: IVP Books, 2008). A classic: Hoyt L. Hickman, Don E. Saliers, Laurence Hull Stookey, and James F. White, *The New Handbook of the Christian Year* (Nashville: Abingdon Press, 1992).

9. The Sunday honoring Christ the Cosmic Ruler (Proper 29, 34) immediately precedes the First Sunday of Advent. While the Gospel text for Year A is the final apocalyptic judgment (Matt. 25:31-46), the texts for Years B and C are from the trial and death of Jesus (John 18:33-37; Luke 23:33-43) and thus call attention to the fact that Jesus' rule is not shallow triumphalism but comes from brutal confrontation with the rulers of the old age. While this makes an important theological point, parishioners often need an explanation for why we come to the climax of the Christian year—which has been building toward the second coming—and then read from the crucifixion.

10. Christian theology after the Bible places much greater emphasis on the

birth of Jesus than do the Gospels and Letters. Mark shows no interest in the birth. Paul does draw on the preexistence of Jesus and his descent from heaven but does not dwell on the birth or life of Jesus. Paul focuses instead on Jesus' death, resurrection, and return. In both Matthew and Luke-Acts, the birth of Jesus is a very small part of the overall books. John gives the fullest theological significance to Jesus as the preexistent Word who becomes flesh. None of these writers—even John—fully articulates the doctrine of the incarnation that comes to expression in later Christian thinking.

11. For a bibliography on Christian practice, see chap. 9, nn. 5, 6, 7, 9.

12. From time to time, occasions and questions come into view that prompt the church to evaluate elements of its fundamental convictions.

13. Each of these theological families is discussed in Ronald J. Allen, *Thinking Theologically: The Preacher as Theologian*. Elements of Preaching (Minneapolis: Fortress Press, 2008).

14. Of course, preachers and congregations who subscribe to the Christian year without the *Revised Common Lectionary* can certainly bring the story of Israel to the attention of the congregation. But the Christian year itself does not require such acquaintance.

15. Latin Hymn, "O Come, O Come, Emmanuel," in *Chalice Hymnal* (St. Louis: Chalice Press, 1995), 119. Preachers sometimes take the name "Israel" as not limited to the Jewish people but as a symbol for all who long for redemption. Even when so interpreted, the raw use of the name "Israel" here suggests negative associations with historical Israel and with contemporary Jewish people.

16. A. Allan McArthur, *The Christian Year and Lectionary Reform* (London: SCM Press, 1958), 68–91.

17. Norman C. Habel, David Rhoads, H. Paul Santmire, eds., *The Season of Creation: A Preaching Commentary* (Minneapolis: Fortress Press, 2011).

18. Timothy Matthew Slemmons, *Year D: A Quadrennial Supplement to the Revised Common Lectionary* (Eugene: Cascade Books, 2012), 38–63.

19. For a description of Year D, see ibid. 64–116.

20. A recent suggestion is to add twenty-two Holy Days of Justice to the Christian Year. Each day focuses on an issue, person, or event important to social justice, such as World AIDS Day, Universal Declaration of Human Rights Day, Martin Luther King Jr. Day, Asian American Heritage Day, International Women's Day, Oscar Romero of the Americas Day, Holocaust Remembrance Day: Yom haShoa. See Dale P. Andrews, Dawn Ottoni-Wilhelm, and Ronald J. Allen, eds., *Preaching God's Transforming Justice: A Lectionary Commentary, Featuring 22 New Holy Days for Justice* (Louisville: Westminster John Knox Press: Year A, 2013, Year B, 2012, Year C 2011).

21. On the RCL readings leading to Christ the Cosmic Ruler and the First Sunday in Advent, see p. 157, n. 4.

22. For a popular survey of such possibilities, see Ronald J. Allen, *A Faith of*

Your Own: Naming What You Really Believe (Louisville: Westminster John Knox Press, 2008), 69–82.

2. Preaching from the *Revised Common Lectionary*: Strengths

1. A concise overview of issues in the history of reconstructing the history of the lectionary is still John Reumann, "A History of Lectionaries from the Synagogue at Nazareth to Post-Vatican II," *Interpretation* 31, no. 2 (1977): 116–30.

2. Paul either commands or presupposes that his letters would be read aloud. See, for example, 1 Thess. 5:27; 1 Cor. 5:9-13; 2 Cor. 1:13; 10:9-10. Cf. Col. 4:16; 2 Pet. 3:15-16.

3. Justin Martyr, *First Apology* 67 in *Early Christian Fathers,* Library of Christian Classics, ed. Cyril C. Richardson, et. al. (Philadelphia: Westminster Press, 1953).

4. For a brief and balanced history of lectionaries, see Gail R. O'Day and Charles Hackett, *Preaching the Revised Common Lectionary* (Nashville: Abingdon Press, 2007), 1–16.

5. The key source is The Consultation on Common Texts, *The Revised Common Lectionary* (Nashville: Abingdon Press, 1992). On assets of the lectionary, the following are especially helpful: Eugene L. Lowry, *Living with the Lectionary: Preaching through the Revised Common Lectionary* (Nashville: Abingdon Press, 1992), 26–36; Fritz West, *Scripture and Memory: The Ecumenical Hermeneutic of the Three-Year Lectionaries* (Collegeville, MN: The Liturgical Press, 1997); Gail Ramshaw, *A Three-Year Banquet* (Minneapolis: Augsburg Fortress, 2004); O'Day and Hackett, *Preaching the Revised Common Lectionary*, 41–47.

6. The Consultation on Common Texts, *The Revised Common Lectionary,* 12–18.

7. Ibid., 12–13.

8. The lectionary also contains readings from three books in the Apocrypha that are read as sacred scripture in some churches: Wisdom of Solomon, Sirach (also known as Ecclesiasticus or Ben Sira), and Baruch.

9. The only books missing from the Torah, Prophets, and Writings in the lectionary are 1 and 2 Chronicles, Obadiah, Nahum, and Zephaniah. The only books missing from the Gospels and Letters are 2 and 3 John, and Jude.

10. The Protestant canon includes only a few either written or given their present form from 400 BCE to the time of Jesus (Jon., Job, Joel, 1 and 2 Chron., Zech. 9–14, Ps., Prov., Song of Sol., Eccles., Esth., Dan. 7–12). As noted in n. 8, Roman Catholic, Anglican, and Eastern churches recognize as sacred scripture some books from the period 400 BCE to the time of Jesus that are not included in the Protestant canon. Without opening the question of what books should be included in the canon, I note that the latter churches have better exposure to the history of

Judaism from Sarah and Abraham to Jesus and the church than do congregations that read only from the Protestant canon.

11. The voices of the Elohist and the Yahwist are embedded in material edited by the priests and the Deuteronomistic theologians. For a classification of the voices in the Torah, Prophets, and Writings, see Ronald J. Allen and John C. Holbert, *Holy Root, Holy Branches: Christian Preaching from the Old Testament* (Nashville: Abingdon Press, 1995), 38–58, 66–67. Apocalyptic theology governs most of the letters (including those of Paul and his followers), the synoptic Gospels, and the book of Revelation. The Johannine literature and Hebrews are largely influenced by Hellenistic Judaism. For comparison and contrast of theologies in the Gospels and Letters influenced by apocalypticism and Hellenistic Judaism, see Ronald J. Allen, *The Life of Jesus for Today* (Louisville: Westminster John Knox, 2008). These seven classifications are not hard-and-fast. Writers in one theological family sometimes incorporate themes from other families.

12. http://www.seasonsonline.ca/412/the_seasons_family_of_resources// (accessed January 15, 2013).

13. The best resource for long-range planning with an eye toward how sermons can interact with one another and can have a cumulative impact is the splendid work by O. Wesley Allen Jr., *Preaching and Reading the Lectionary; A Three Dimension Approach to the Liturgical Year* (St. Louis: Chalice Press, 2007).

14. The classic guide to such groups is still John S. McClure, *The Roundtable Pulpit: Where Preaching and Leadership Meet* (Nashville: Abingdon Press, 1995).

3. Preaching from the *Revised Common Lectionary*: Cautions

1. The following are among helpful analyses of the liabilities of the lectionary: James A. Sanders, "Canon and Calendar," in Dieter Hessel, ed., *Social Teaching of the Christian Year* (Philadelphia: Geneva Press, 1983), 257–63; Eugene L. Lowry, *Living with the Lectionary: Preaching Through the Revised Common Lectionary* (Nashville: Abingdon Press, 1992), 16–25; Shelley Cochran, *The Pastor's Underground Guide to the Revised Common Lectionary* (St. Louis: Chalice Press, 1995, 1996, 1997), esp. 1995: 1–33; Timothy Matthew Slemmons, *Year D: A Quadrennial Supplement to the Revised Common Lectionary* (Eugene; Cascade Books, 2012), 1–38.

2. The best discussion of otherness in the literature of preaching is John S. McClure, *Other-wise Preaching: A Postmodern Ethic for Homiletics* (St. Louis: Chalice Press, 2001). A junior introduction is Ronald J. Allen, *Preaching and the Other: Studies of Postmodern Insights* (St. Louis: Chalice Press, 2009), 28–46.

3. Ordinary Time presses a less predetermined theological lens on the Bible readings than do the two cycles focused almost completely on redemption. The continuous and semi-continuous readings of the letters and the Torah, Prophets, and Writings are among the biblical materials least defined by the categories of the Christian year.

4. The Christian year and the lectionary themselves can be other to those outside Christian faith, as well as to those within Christian community who have not encountered the Christian year. Some congregations who have regularly observed the Christian year experience it afresh when their circumstances change.

5. For a fuller and more trenchant discussion, see Ronald J. Allen and John C. Holbert, *Holy Root, Holy Branches: Christian Preaching from the Old Testament* (Nashville: Abingdon Press, 1995), 132–51.

6. On theological malaise, I still stand with my early statements: Clark M. Williamson and Ronald J. Allen, *The Teaching Minister* (Louisville: Westminster John Knox Press, 1991), 11–25 and Ronald J. Allen, *The Teaching Sermon* (Nashville: Abingdon Press, 1995), 13–25.

7. Thomas G. Bandy offers an intriguing attempt to rethink the relationship between the Bible and preaching (and worship) from the standpoint of becoming more inviting and missional in his *Introducing the Uncommon Lectionary: Opening the Bible to Seekers and Disciples* (Nashville: Abingdon Press, 2006).

4. Preaching through a Book of the Bible (Continuous Lectionary)

1. Preachers sometimes conflate continuous preaching with verse-by-verse preaching. While continuous preaching today is sometimes associated with verse-by-verse preaching, the two are not inherently related. Continuous peaching can take place in any form, including verse by verse. Verse-by-verse preaching can be employed in connection with any biblical starting point for preaching, including *lectio continua, lectio selecta,* and texts chosen freely. A work that considers preaching verse by verse: Ronald J. Allen and Gilbert L. Bartholomew, *Preaching Verse by Verse* (Louisville: Westminster John Knox Press, 2000).

2. For further discussion of continuous and semi-continuous preaching from the lectionary, see pp. 33, 43, 49–51.

3. Hughes Oliphant Old gives a reverential account of the history of continuous preaching in his *Worship: Reformed according to Scripture*, revised and expanded ed. (Louisville: Westminster John Knox Press, 2002), 59–90; and in his larger *The Reading and Preaching of the Scriptures in the Worship of the Christian Church* (Grand Rapids: Eerdmans, 1998), vol. 1, 100–101, 246–48, 314–15, 344–45; vol. 2 (1998): 36, 51, 112–14, 138, 150–51, 159, 173, 214, 284, 287–88, 292, 294–95, 316, 327, 340, 419, 438; vol. 3 (1999): 43, 78, 83, 85, 109, 156–58, 164, 167, 173, 176–78, 308, 363–64, 365–80, 389.

4. See further Michael H. Marlowe, "English Translations of the Aramaic Targums," http://www.bible-researcher.com/aramaic5.html (accessed December 2, 2012).

5. The Talmud was given its present form about the sixth century CE, but it contains much older traditions.

6. See H. Freedman and Maurice Simon, eds., *Midrash Rabbah* (London:

Soncino Press, 1939), 10 volumes; W. G. Braude, ed., *The Midrash on Psalms*, Yale Judaica series (New Haven: Yale University Press, 1959), 2 volumes.

7. See Old, *Worship Reformed according to Scripture*, esp. 61, 66–68, 70–71, 73–74, 82, 84–87, 172; and *The Reading and Preaching of the Scriptures in the Worship of the Christian Church*, vol. 4 (2002), 27, 31, 33, 36–37, 46–47, 51, 60, 63–64, 68–69, 70, 77, 85, 94–96, 152–55, 205–7, 257, 260, 284, 327, 374, 413–15, 420, 459.

8. An excellent and easily accessible resource for semi-continuous preaching is *The Narrative Lectionary* sponsored by the Center for Biblical Preaching in connection with Workingpreacher.org at Luther Seminary. The notion of "narrative" here refers not to a literary genre but to following the unfolding story of the Bible. In the fall, *The Narrative Lectionary* summarizes the biblical story from Genesis to the coming of Jesus. In the winter, the lectionary follows one Gospel. In the spring this table of readings focuses on the church in Acts and in the Letters. http://www.workingpreacher.org/narrative_lectionary.aspx (accessed December 21, 2012).

9. While the story of Gideon needs to be preached as a whole, this section is too long to be read in entirety as a scripture lesson in public worship. The preacher needs to choose sections to represent the whole. These things are also true in connection with the following sermons from Judg. 13:1–16:31 and Judg. 20:1–21:25.

5. Preaching from the African American Lectionary and Other Cultural and Civic Calendars

1. The primary source for following the African American Lectionary is http://theafricanamericanlectionary.org/ (accessed January 15, 2013).

2. For 2011 through 2014, collaborative partners publishing this journal are The African American Pulpit, Inc. (for which Martha Simmons is president), American Baptist College of Nashville (Forrest Harris, President); the Lilly Endowment continues to fund the project.

3. "The Lectionary Team," The African American Lectionary, accessed January 15, 2013, http://theafricanamericanlectionary.org/about.asp.

4. See pp. 49–62 in this book.

5. This theme is elaborated in chap. 8, pp. 129–33.

6. Ronald J. Allen, "The Church as Community of Conversation," in *Under the Oak Tree: The Church as Community of Conversation in a Conflicted and Pluralistic World,* eds. O. Wesley Allen Jr., John S. McClure, and Ronald J. Allen (Eugene: Cascade Books, forthcoming, 2013).

7. A. Allan McArthur, *The Christian Year and Lectionary Reform* (London: SCM Press, 1958): 68–91.

8. Norman C. Habel, David Rhoads, H. Paul Santmire, eds., *The Season of Creation: A Preaching Commentary* (Minneapolis: Fortress Press, 2011).

9. Timothy Matthew Slemmons, *Year D: A Quadrennial Supplement to the Revised Common Lectionary* (Eugene: Cascade Books, 2012), 38–63.

10. For a description of Year D, see ibid., 64–116.

11. Dale P. Andrews, Dawn Ottoni-Wilhelm, and Ronald J. Allen, eds., *Preaching God's Transforming Justice: A Lectionary Commentary, Featuring 22 New Holy Days for Justice* (Louisville: Westminster John Knox Press: Year A, 2013, Year B, 2012, Year C 2011).

6. Preaching from the Chronology of the Bible and from Schools of Thought within the Bible

1. As noted on pp. 33, 39, 43–44, contemporary theological groups disagree on the extent and kinds of diversity in the Bible. Theological households who acknowledge the Bible as the only authority in the church see the content of the different writings as entirely cohesive. For them, diversity is largely a matter of expression. The preacher needs to acquaint the congregation with the different forms of biblical literature and with how to apply the different theologies to life today. At the other end of the theological spectrum, some theological families believe the Bible contains different theologies. The preacher needs to help the congregation identify these theologies, and their strengths and weaknesses, and to help the congregation enter conversation with them. A simplified version of these approaches and their consequences for biblical interpretation and theological reflection is worked out in Ronald J. Allen, *Reading the Bible for the First Time* (Grand Rapids: Eerdmans, 2012), 167–85.

2. James A. Sanders, "Canon and Calendar: An Alternative Lectionary Proposal," in *Social Themes of the Christian Year,* ed. Dieter T. Hessel (Philadelphia: Geneva Press, 1983), 257–63.

3. Scholars often distinguish between the historical figures and events and the interpretation of those figures and events in their present form in the Bible. For example, we might distinguish between the historical Moses and Moses as depicted in the Deuteronomistic or priestly theologies or between the historical Jesus and Jesus as he is portrayed in each of the Gospels. If the preacher has access to reliable reconstructions of historical biblical figures and events, the preacher might preach from those events. It is sometimes instructive to the congregation for the preacher to trace how Israel or the church interpreted and reinterpreted a particular figure, idea, or event.

4. The preacher can easily identify the Deuteronomistic, priestly, wisdom, end-time, and Hellenistic Jewish perspectives because they largely exist in biblical books that voice their theology, for example, Deuteronomy. The Elohist and Yahwist voices are now embedded in other bodies of literature and do not exist as distinct books. Some scholars do not embrace this idea.

5. For an exposition of this early tradition, see Bernhard W. Anderson with Steven Bishop and Judith H. Newman, *Understanding the Old Testament,* 5th ed. (Saddle River, NJ: Pearson Prentice Hall, 2007), 141–66. Different scholars construe this history in different ways.

6. Richard Elliott Friedman provides a color-coded translation of the Penta-teuch that shows the different sources (Yahwist, Elohist, Deuteronomistic, and priestly) in different colors in his *The Bible with Sources Revealed: A New Way into the Five Books of Moses* (San Francisco: HarperSanFrancisco, 2003). Scholars some-times disagree on how to classify particular passages.

7. On the Yahwist: Anderson, *Understanding the Old Testament,* 140, 145, 226–27, 410. For a popular introduction: Richard Elliott Friedman, *Who Wrote the Bible?* (New York: Simon and Schuster, 1987), 50–100.

8. Anderson's exposition of the Elohist is not as satisfactory as the other view-points, though; see pp. 22, 152, 158, 289–90. For a fuller explication, see Fried-man, *Who Wrote the Bible?* Esp. 70–100.

9. On Deuteronomism, see Anderson, *Understanding the Old Testament,* 324–54, 409–10

10. On this perspective a general introduction is Anderson, *Understanding the Old Testament,* 409–24. Cf. 389–409, 425–55.

11. For a general overview, see Anderson, *Understanding the Old Testament,* 519–52. Still luminous is James L. Crenshaw, *Old Testament Wisdom: An Introduc-tion* (Atlanta: John Knox Press, 1981).

12. On apocalyptic: Anderson, *Understanding the Old Testament,* 573–87; Ronald J. Allen, *The Life of Jesus for Today,* For Today Series (Louisville: Westmin-ster John Knox Press, 2008), 19–28.

13. For an overview, see Ronald J. Allen, *The Life of Jesus for Today,* 82–90.

14. For an expansion of this approach in connection with the Gospels and Letters, see Ronald J. Allen, *Reading the New Testament for the First Time* (Grand Rapids: Eerdmans, 2012), 37–53.

7. Preaching a Series That Starts with the Bible

1. For a practical approach to sermon series, see *Circuit Rider,* February/March/April 2013, focused on "The Ultimate Sermon Series."

2. An alternate approach to such a series would be to look at the different motifs of covenant in the theological families discussed in the previous chapter: the Mosaic covenant in the period of the national epic, the Yahwists, the Deu-teronomistic theology, the priestly theology, Wisdom, end-time theologies, and Hellenistic Judaism.

8. Preaching from Doctrines, Practices, and Personal and Social Issues

1. Topical preaching is rarely discussed in the literature of preaching today. Here are three resources: Ronald J. Allen, *Preaching the Topical Sermon* (Louisville:

Westminster John Knox Press, 1992); and Jane Rzepka and Ken Sawyer, *Thematic Preaching* (St. Louis: Chalice Press, 2001); David Buttrick, *Homiletic* (Philadelphia: Fortress Press, 1987), 405–48.

2. Among resources for preaching on doctrine: Robert G. Hughes and Robert Kysar, *Preaching Doctrine for the Twenty-First Century,* Fortress Resources for Preaching (Minneapolis: Fortress Press, 2009); William J Carl III, *Preaching Christian Doctrine* (Minneapolis: Fortress Press, 2008); Robert Smith, *Doctrine That Dances: Bringing Doctrinal Preaching and Teaching to Life* (Nashville: B&H Academic Publishing, 2008). A scholar of preaching who has given unusual attention to doctrine is Paul Scott Wilson, esp. *Imagination of the Heart: New Understandings in Preaching* (Nashville: Abingdon Press, 1988); and *The Practice of Preaching,* rev. ed. (Nashville: Abingdon Press, 2007), 225–26, 237–42; and his edited series, *Abingdon Theological Commentary to the Lectionary* (Nashville: Abingdon Press, 2012: Year C; 2013: Year A; 2014: Year B).

3. On the relationship between doctrine and theology in preaching: Ronald J. Allen, *Preaching Is Believing: The Sermon as Theological Reflection* (Louisville: Westminster John Knox Press, 2002).

4. On these theological families see Ronald J. Allen, *Thinking Theologically: The Preacher as Theologian,* Elements of Preaching Series (Minneapolis: Fortress Press, 2008).

5. On this general phenomenon, see Allen, *Preaching Is Believing,* passim.

6. The classic discussion of practice is Alisdair MacIntyre, *After Virtue,* 2nd ed. (Notre Dame: University of Notre Dame Press, 1984), esp. 187. For broader understandings of practice: Miraslav Volf and Dorothy C. Bass, eds., *Practicing Theology: Beliefs and Practices in Christian Life* (Grand Rapids: Eerdmans, 2002). An exceptionally crisp summary of Christian practice is found at http://www.practicingourfaith.org/what-are-christian-practices (accessed February 13, 2013).

7. E. Bryon Anderson, *Worship and Christian Identity: Practicing Ourselves* (Collegeville, MN: Liturgical Press, 2003).

8. On preaching as a practice and the teaching of preaching as also a Christian practice, see Thomas G. Long and Leonora Tubbs Tisdale, *Teaching Preaching as a Christian Practice: A New Approach to Homiletical Pedagogy* (Louisville: Westminster John Knox Press, 2008). On the practice of giving testimony: Thomas G. Long, *Testimony: Talking Ourselves into Being Christian,* The Practices of Faith Series (San Francisco: Jossey-Bass, 2004).

9. Dorothy C. Bass, ed., *Practicing Our Faith: A Way of Life for a Searching People,* The Practices of Faith Series, 2nd ed. (San Francisco: Jossey-Bass, 2010); and Craig Dykstra, *Growing in the Life of Faith: Education and Christian Practices* (Louisville: Westminster John Knox Press, 1999), 27–28.

10. David Schnasa Jacobsen and Robert Allen Kelley provide a model for thinking and preaching theologically about "commonplaces," that is, particular situations that recur in life: *Kairos Preaching: Speaking the Gospel to the Situation* (Minneapolis: Fortress Press, 2009).

11. Ronald J. Allen, Dale P. Andrews, Dawn Ottoni-Wilhelm, *Preaching God's Transforming Justice: A Lectionary Commentary Featuring 22 New Holy Days for Justice: Years A, B, and C* (Louisville: Westminster John Knox Press, 2011, 2012, 2013), xxii.

9. Preaching from a Free Selection of Biblical Texts or Themes

1. This chapter focuses on freely selecting individual biblical texts. Ministers can also freely select—and preach on—biblical themes, that is, a theme that develops across several biblical passages or books. The perspectives in this chapter apply to freely chosen themes as well as passages. On themes, see Ronald J. Allen, *Wholly Scripture: Preaching Biblical Themes* (St. Louis: Chalice Press, 2004); and Allen, *Preaching Luke-Acts,* Preaching Classic Texts (St. Louis: Chalice Press, 2000).

2. When a one-shot assignment takes the preacher to a church or setting that follows the Christian year and the lectionary, the preacher would take the text or theme from the readings assigned for that day. I am working here with occasions when preachers can select their own texts. Some of the things to take in account articulated here also apply to one-shot assignments in lectionary-based settings.

CPSIA information can be obtained at www.ICGtesting.com
Printed in the USA
LVOW13s1346101013

356209LV00005B/10/P